Ancient Egypt: Foundations of a Civilization

Ancient Egypt: Foundations of a Civilization

Douglas J. Brewer

PEARSON
Longman

Harlow, England • London • New York • Boston • San Francisco • Toronto
Sydney • Tokyo • Singapore • Hong Kong • Seoul • Taipei • New Delhi
Cape Town • Madrid • Mexico City • Amsterdam • Munich • Paris • Milan

PEARSON EDUCATION LIMITED

Edinburgh Gate
Harlow CM20 2JE
United Kingdom
Tel: +44 (0)1279 623623
Fax: +44 (0)1279 431059
Website: www.pearsoned.co.uk

First edition published in Great Britain in 2005

© Pearson Education Limited 2005

The right of Douglas Brewer to be identified as author
of this work has been asserted by him in accordance
with the Copyright, Designs and Patents Act 1988.

ISBN-13: 978–0–58277–253–3
ISBN-10: 0–58277–253–2

British Library Cataloguing in Publication Data
A CIP catalogue record for this book can be obtained from the British Library

Library of Congress Cataloging in Publication Data
A CIP catalog record for this book can be obtained from the Library of Congress

10   9   8   7   6   5   4   3   2   1
09   08   07   06   05

Set in 9.5/14pt Melior by 35
Printed and bound in China
CTPSc/01

The Publishers' policy is to use paper manufactured from sustainable forests.

Contents

List of figures, boxes and plates

Figures

Boxes

Plates

(In central plate section)

Acknowledgements

I am thankful and deeply appreciative of all who helped in the writing and production of this volume. It would be impossible to name everyone who assisted me, but a number of individuals deserve special thanks – most notable are Jeremy Geller, University of Illinois; Patricia Spencer and the Egypt Exploration Society; Kellie Leydon and the British Museum; Hugh Kilmister of the Petrie Museum; Mindy McNaugher of the Carnegie Museum of Natural History; Art Resources Inc.; Cleveland Museum of Art; Brooklyn Museum of Art; and the Spurlock Museum. Patrick Carstens deserves a special note of thanks for allowing me to use so many of his wonderful photographs of Egypt. Brenda Coelho and Loren Kirkwood composed the many graphics included here. Several chapters are based on an earlier work co-authored with Emily Teeter. Dr Teeter's contribution to that work and consequently to this effort are reflected in those sections related to religion, lifestyles and language (writing). Other chapters too are undoubtedly a product of our long constructive conversations on a variety of topics. I am also most grateful to Ann Hutflies Brewer who provided valuable insights and structure to the earlier chapters and to Beth Watkins and the anonymous third editor and two reviewers who survived the painstaking chore of reading earlier versions of this work and offering valuable editorial opinions. Finally a thank you is due to Belinda and the morning crew at the Bayside on Orcas Island for plying me with coffee and breakfast sundries through the long writing and editing phase.

Publisher's acknowledgements

We are grateful to the following for permission to reproduce copyright material:

Cambridge University Press for Tables 1.1 and 2.1, from Brewer, Douglas J., and Teeter, Emily, *Egypt and the Egyptians* (Cambridge University Press, 1999); Thompson Publishing Services for Table 2.2, from Wilkinson, Toby A. H., *Early Dynastic Egypt* (Routledge, 1999).

Figures 1.3, 4.4, 4.7, 4.10, 6.6, 6.15, 6.20 and 9.10 courtesy of the Spurlock Museum, University of Illinois; Figure 2.1 courtesy of Erich Lessing/Art Resource, NY, Musee des Beaux-Arts, Lille, France; Figure 3.1a courtesy of Erich Lessing/Art Resource, NY. Oriental Institute, University of Chicago; Figure 3.1b courtesy of Erich Lessing/Art Resource, NY. Saggara, Egypt; Figures 3.4, 3.5, 3.10, 5.1a, 5.1b, 5.3, 10.12 courtesy of Patrick Richard Carstens; Figures 3.9, 6.2 and 10.9b from Brewer, Douglas J., and Teeter, Emily, *Egypt and the Egyptians* (Cambridge University Press, 1999); Figures 4.5, 4.9, 6.4d, 6.9, 6.18, 6.19 and 9.5a © Copyright the British Museum; Figures 5.2, 5.4, 6.4a, 6.4b, 6.5, 6.7, 6.14, 9.6, 9.11, 10.3, 10.5, 10.7, 10.8c and 10.8d courtesy of the Egypt Exploration Society; Figure 6.8 from Petrie, W. M. F., *Naqada and Ballas* (Aris and Phillips, 1974) and Figures 6.1 and 9.14 from Brewer, Douglas, Redford, Donald and Redford, Susan, *Domestic Plants and Animals: The Egyptian Origins* (Aris and Phillips, 1991), courtesy of Oxbow Books; Figures 6.10, 6.11, 6.12, 6.14, 6.21, 6.23, 8.6, 8.11 and 9.5b Copyright Petrie Museum of Egyptian Archaeology, University College London; Figures 6.13, 6.18, 6.22, 6.25, 6.26, 8.8a courtesy of the Brooklyn Museum of Art; Figure 6.16 from Aldred, C. A., *Egypt to the End of the Old Kingdom*, 1965, courtesy of Thames and Hudson; Figures 6.17, 8.4a, 9.13 and 10.4 courtesy of Jeremy Geller; Figures 7.3, 7.6a and 7.6b courtesy of Werner Forman/ Art Resources, NY. Ashmolean Museum. Oxford; Figure 7.6c courtesy of David George; Figure 7.7 courtesy of Erich Lessing/Art Resource, NY, Louvre, Paris; Figure 8.1 from Lehner, Mark, *The Complete Pyramids*, 1997 (Thames and Hudson Ltd, London, 1997); Figure 8.3 courtesy of Réunion des Musées Nationaux/Art Resources, NY, Louvre, Paris; Figure 8.5 courtesy of Erich Lessing/Art Resource, NY; Figures 8.7, 8.8b and 10.2b from Spencer, A. J., *Early Egypt: The Rise of Civilisation in the Nile Valley*, courtesy of the Trustees of the British Museum; Figure 8.10a courtesy of Jean Vertut "L'art de l'ancienne Egypte" – Citadelles & Mazenod, Jean Vertut "L'art de l'ancienne Egypte" – Citadelles & Mazenod, Paris; Figure 8.10b courtesy of Werner Forman/Art Resources, NY. Egyptian Museum Cairo; Figure 10.9 courtesy of Jean Mazenod "L'art de l'ancienne Egypte" – Citadelles & Mazenod, Jean Vertut "L'art de l'ancienne Egypte" – Citadelles & Mazenod, Paris Figure 9.1 from Baines, John and Malek, Jaromir *Atlas of Ancient Egypt* (Phaidon, 1980), courtesy of Lovell Johns; Figure 9.12 courtesy of Erich Lessing/Art Resource, NY. Tomb of Nakht, Thebes, Egypt; Figures 10.2c, 10.2d and 10.2e courtesy of Bernard Bothmer; Figure 10.8a Courtesy of Scala/Art Resource, NY.

Plates 1, 8, 9 and 18 courtesy of the Carnegie Museum of Natural History; Plates 3, 5 and 29 courtesy of Patrick Richard Carstens; Plates 10, 11, 12, 13, 14, 15, 16, 17, 22 and 30 copyright the Petrie Museum of Egyptian Archaeology, University College London; Plates 19 and 20 courtesy of the Cleveland Museum of Art, Gift of the John Huntingdon Art and Polytechnic Trust; Plates 21 and 24 courtesy of the Brooklyn Museum of Art; Plate 23 © Copyright the British Museum; Plates 7, 26 and 27 courtesy of the Egypt Exploration Society.

In some instances we have been unable to trace the owners of copyright material, and we would appreciate any information that would enable us to do so.

To Rachel Marina and Joseph William, for simply being themselves.

Introduction

As many readers are no doubt aware, the number of books written about Dynastic Egypt – the period beginning about 2700 BC with the erection of the first pyramid and ending with Cleopatra's infamous encounter with an asp in 30 BC – might easily fill the public library of most small towns. On the other hand, those books dealing with the period predating the great pharaohs would hardly fill a single library shelf. Yet some of the most fundamental and fascinating aspects of later Egyptian civilisation can only be understood by looking deep into Egypt's past. Egypt's prehistoric culture provided the foundation for all later periods of Egyptian civilisation. Pyramids, hieroglyphic writing, belief in the afterlife and fervent nationalism – indeed all the hallmarks of classic Egyptian culture and even many aspects of modern Egyptian culture – can be traced in an unbroken line back to Egypt's earliest peoples.

The ancient Egyptians themselves held their prehistoric and Early Dynastic past in great esteem, and they were well aware of its importance in defining and understanding their world. As the ancient Egyptians sought to understand their present by knowing their past, we too can gain insight and understanding of Egyptian culture through knowledge of its formative era, knowledge that can turn seemingly contradictory cultural beliefs and other 'mysteries' into understandable practices.

Unfortunately, not only are a limited number of books written about this period, very few are directed to the non-specialist. The goal of this book is to fill this void. Although written for the non-specialist, this book presents current research on Egyptian origins, focusing on three broad topics: (a) the connection between environment and culture, (b) the formation of agricultural communities and (c) the rise of the nation-state.

A basic review of the fields of Egyptology and archaeology, as well as an overview of Egypt's Prehistoric Period (Chapters 1 and 2), is critical to understanding later developments, and thus we begin our journey here. Because Egypt's environment is reflected throughout the ancient culture from daily life to hieroglyphs to regional politics, we next tour the Nile Valley's varied landscapes (Chapter 3) and then meet its earliest inhabitants and learn how they lived (Chapter 4). This period, the Paleolithic (or Old Stone Age), and the later Neolithic (or New Stone Age) introduce us to the first 'Egyptians' and end by setting the stage for the rise of agriculture and village life (Chapter 5). Chapters 6 and 7 detail the artistic motifs and artefacts recovered from early population centres of Pre- and Protodynastic Egypt and explain how these early forms evolved into the familiar symbols and material culture of classic Egyptian civilisation.

How exactly Egypt coalesced into a single nation still remains unclear, but recent investigations have been shedding some light on the processes surrounding unification (Chapter 7). One fruitful avenue of study is the geographic location of certain population centres, which may have provided the stimulus for the quest for power and riches. The search for the identity of the first pharaoh (Chapter 8) also offers clues as to how the Egyptian state emerged and became the world's first regional super-power.

Chapter 9 describes everyday life in the ancient nation-state, while the crowning achievement of early formative Egypt – the building of the first pyramids – is discussed in Chapter 10. All the advances of the formative period – agriculture, irrigation, writing, political organisation and nation building – culminate in the creation of these fitting monuments to the glory of early Egypt.

CHAPTER 1

Archaeology, Egyptology and prehistory: How we know what we know

Archaeology and its development

A rchaeology is an accepted and popular social science taught in universities around the world. As a discipline, archaeology tries to explain what has happened to specific groups of humans in the past and what processes are involved when cultures experience change. Yet, unlike cultural anthropologists, geographers, sociologists and scholars in other related fields of study, archaeologists cannot observe the behaviour of the people they are investigating, nor do they have direct access to the thoughts of these people as recorded in written texts as do the historians. Instead, archeologists can only infer human behaviour and ideas from the materials these people left behind. Materials are recovered by surveying and excavating, then analysed within the context of the associated environment. Most archaeologists' hypotheses are based solely on recovered artefacts, which they have identified by comparisons to known pieces, hoping that similarity in appearance equates to similarity in function. Technical studies, such as the study of wear patterns, can often augment archaeologists' comparative analogies by demonstrating how ancient tools were used, thereby providing clues as to their function (scraping, cutting, etc.). Simple logic and references to other known objects of similar design, more often than not, serve as archaeologists' only means of identification. Naturally, such interpretations are always open to debate and revision and thus underscore the need for archaeologists to publish their results so that additional comparisons and refinements can be made after further discoveries.

Although most cultures throughout time have shown an interest in their past, archaeology as a discipline has its roots in the Italian Renaissance, when fourteenth-century scholars began to question the origins of the ancient Classical monuments located throughout the Mediterranean region. It was clear that they were built by a civilisation prior to Renaissance Europe that in many ways rivalled or even surpassed it. Europeans began travelling to other lands, particularly the Near East and Classical world, to retrieve ancient objects for their governments' museums or simply to profit from the sale of the pieces. Thus began a collecting spree that continues, at least to some degree, today.

Others with an interest in the past (and who were often spurred on by a nationalistic ideology) turned their eyes to the mounds and monuments within the borders of their own countries. Though neither as overtly spectacular nor as easily recovered as the material remains of the ancient Mediterranean cultures, the artefacts and sites of northern Europe did yield tantalising clues to their ancient makers when subjected to careful study. It was this line of discovery, characterised by painstaking recovery and meticulous documentation, that laid the foundation for the scientific discipline known today as archaeology.

But there were still crucial developments that needed to take place in the fields of geology, biology and the social sciences before modern archaeology could be born. The first of these was the publication of Charles Lyell's *Principles of Geology* from 1830 to 1833, which demonstrated the Earth's great antiquity and broke the so-called biblical time

---

BOX 1.1 ◆ The biblical time barrier

Based on genealogies listed in the biblical book of Genesis, seventeenth-century Archbishop Ussher computed the world's age to be less than 6,000 years old. He went on to establish a date of 4004 BC for the Earth's creation.

barrier for the world's creation. Building on previous work by Cuvier and Hutton, and using evidence he gathered in the region around Mount Etna, Lyell stressed that there are natural (as opposed to supernatural) explanations for all geological phenomena, that the ordinary natural processes of today do not differ in kind or magnitude from those of the past, and that the Earth must therefore be very ancient because these processes work so slowly. Though these concepts may seem obvious to us today, they were revolutionary in Lyell's time. In addition to laying out the methods and principles that modern geologists use every day, Lyell's *Principles of Geology* provided a younger group of scholars the opportunity to speculate on time and change.

One of those most profoundly influenced by Lyell's work was a young scientist named Charles Darwin. Darwin's biological treatise *Origin of Species*, published in 1859, expounded on the diversity of life and described evolutionary change through time. Simply put, he believed that those groups of living organisms best adjusted to the conditions in which they lived had the greatest chance for survival and passing on their traits to the next generation. By applying the same principle to human culture, scholars now had a mechanism by which to explain why peoples of the past and their societies differed from contemporary ones.

These two concepts – the great antiquity of the Earth and natural selection – were quickly applied to human and extinct animal remains found in the Somme Valley of France, and for the first time scholars began to accept human co-existence with extinct animals, a fact that many people had refused to believe even when confronted with the clear evidence of stone tools lying juxtaposed with ancient bones. In 1869, soon after the acceptance of this co-existence, the first evidence of prehistoric humans in Egypt was reported: stone tools, tens of thousands of years old, found in the Nile Valley.

At the turn of the twentieth century, advances in archaeological methods taking place in the Near East were turning the field from a treasure hunt into a scientific discipline (see Chapter 2). Scholars working in the Americas were particularly influenced by the British archaeologist Sir Flinders Petrie's method of building a chronology using only material remains (i.e. sequence dating or seriation typology; see below and Chapter 2 for detailed explanations of this technique). This was because the indigenous cultures of the Americas either did not have a written language or, as in the case of the Maya, their written language was as yet undecipherable. Thus scholars wanting to create a cultural chronology of the Americas had to do so using pottery or stone tools, because they did not have historical records on which to rely.

Another circumstance that influenced the direction archaeology would take has to do with the disciplines with which the early archaeologists were most closely affiliated. In the Old World, archaeology was basically an outgrowth of history, and the archaeologists were, in general, historians looking at material culture. In the New World, however, archaeologists were more closely affiliated with ethnographers and cultural anthropologists because they were excavating sites that belonged to the direct ancestors of the living peoples whom the anthropologists were studying. Thus, it was perfectly natural for the New World archaeologists to work closely with the anthropologists and borrow their theoretical perspective. At first, this distinction had very little practical impact, as both the historical archaeologists and the anthropological archaeologists were primarily interested in constructing cultural chronologies of their respective regions. By the middle of the twentieth century, however, the two types of archaeology began to diverge. Anthropologists, and by extension anthropological archaeologists, began to focus on questions of process – the 'how' and 'why' of culture change, in addition to the historical questions of 'when' and 'where'.

Today anthropological (or New World) archaeology is fundamentally a generalising and comparative discipline – it begins with the particulars of a human society and culture, but then compares the culture with others in an attempt to highlight similarities and contrast differences. The data compiled by anthropologists and the methods they employ help archaeologists better understand the ways in which a presumably related ancient culture might have functioned and evolved through time. The continuing closeness of these two fields is demonstrated by the fact that in most American universities cultural anthropology (ethnology) and archaeology are both considered disciplinary sub-fields of anthropology.

What, then, is Egyptology and how does it differ from archaeology? Egyptology is a *historical* discipline devoted to the study of ancient Egypt. It is modelled on Classical studies of Greece and Rome, which rely on written records to supply chronology, historical data and information about beliefs of the past. Egyptologists work with specific texts to understand nuances of the ancient culture, often within a well-defined time period. Like all historical disciplines, Egyptology is a particularising discipline. That is, it is primarily interested in defining what happened at a specific place and time.

One could argue that Egyptology began with the Egyptians themselves. There is evidence that ancient Egyptians looked back in time, often in awe of their cultural accomplishments. We know that one of Ramesses II's sons (c.1250 BC) was concerned with the preservation of ancient monuments and worked to clear and identify a number of architectural ruins. The ancient Greeks and Romans were also intrigued by the Egyptians' accomplishments and wrote extensively on what they encountered when travelling there, a culture by then already over 3,000 years old:

> And since Egypt is the country where mythology places the origins of the gods, where the earliest observations of the stars are said to have been made, and where, furthermore, many noteworthy deeds of great men are recorded, we shall begin our history with the events connected with Egypt.
>
> [Diodorus of Sicily, c.58 BC (I:9:9)]

After the Napoleonic wars, Egypt became a protectorate of the British Empire, thereby offering some security to would-be Western travellers. As scholarly works began to be published, Egypt was invaded by adventurers, scholars and artists in a virtual free-for-all to see who could acquire the largest collection of Egypt's antiquities. Jean-François Champollion's publication of translated hieroglyphs (1824), based on his work on the Rosetta Stone, marked the beginning of Egyptology as a scholarly discipline. Continued scholarly pursuits ultimately led to establishing Egyptian–British governmental control over Egypt's antiquities and the curbing of wholesale looting.

Egyptology has an obvious relationship with anthropological archaeology, because both deal with the human past, its narration and its explanation. Some Egyptologists interested in the development of art and architecture employ archaeological techniques to recover objects, but they analyse them within their own historical (not anthropological) theoretical framework. Where Egyptology and archaeology really converge to illuminate the human past is in studies of Predynastic and Early Dynastic

Egypt, when contemporary written records are few in number, selective in subject matter or imperfectly translated, and we need to supplement them with archaeologically recovered artefacts and sites. Anthropological archaeology takes the lead in studies of even earlier time periods in Egypt, before the development of written language. Because of the nature of the remains, generalising anthropological questions – such as how did the domestication of animals, agriculture, nation-state, written language, etc. develop in Egypt and compare with other early cultures – are the focus of studies of Egyptian prehistory.

Chronologies and dating techniques

In order to determine the age of an artefact, Egyptologists and archaeologists working in the historical period rely heavily on the Egyptian dynastic chronology, one of the oldest and most reliable means of affixing a calendrical date to an object or site. A dynasty is a succession of rulers from the same line of descent. (Ideally, kingship was passed from father to son; if no son was available, a brother or son-in-law might rule. When someone unrelated to the previous king ascended to the throne – either by default or through a coup – a new dynasty was created.) The Egyptian chronology is composed of 32 dynasties, beginning in about 3050 BC with Menes (Narmer), Egypt's first ruler, and ending with Cleopatra in 30 BC. Modern scholars have grouped the dynasties into 'kingdoms,' within which many social and political values were shared (Table 1.1).

The origin of the dynastic chronological system dates back to the time of Alexander the Great. After Alexander's death, his empire was divided among his generals, one of whom, Ptolemy, received the richest prize, Egypt. Under his son, Ptolemy II Philadelphus (c.280 BC), an Egyptian priest named Manetho wrote a condensed history of his native land for the new Greek rulers. Manetho, a native of Sebennytus in the Delta, had been educated in the old scribal traditions. Although Egypt's priests were famous for handing out titbits of information (often intentionally incorrect) to curious travellers, none had ever attempted to compile a complete history of Egypt, especially for foreigners.

Manetho's history was, in essence, a chronology of events arranged from oldest to most recent, according to the reign of a particular king. As early as Dynasty 1, years of a king's reign were identified by an important

TABLE 1.1 ◆ *The dynastic sequence as defined by modern acholars (all dates are approximate).*

EARLY DYNASTIC: DYNASTIES 0–3 (3150–2613 BC)

Dynasty 0 (3150–3050 BC)
Scorpion
Ka
Narmer
Dynasty 1 (3050–2890 BC)
Aha
Djer
Djet
Den
Dynasty 2 (2890–2686 BC)
Hetepsekhemiu
Perisbsen
Khasekhemui
Dynasty 3 (2686–2613 BC)
Djoser
Sekhemkhet
Khaba Huni

OLD KINGDOM: DYNASTIES 4–6 (2613–2181 BC)

Dynasty 4 (2613–2498 BC)
Snefru
Khufu
Djedefre
Khafre
Menkaure
Shepseskaf
Dynasty 5 (2498–2345 BC)
Userkaf
Sahure
Neferirare-Kakai
Niuserre
Unis
Dynasty 6 (2345–2181 BC)
Teti
Pepi I
Mernere
Pepi II
Nitocris (?)

FIRST INTERMEDIATE PERIOD: DYNASTIES 7–11 (2181–2040 BC)

Dynasties 7–10 (2181–2160 BC)
Dynasty 11 (2133–2160 BC)
Wahankh Antef II
Mentuhotep I–III

MIDDLE KINGDOM: DYNASTIES 12 and early 13 (2040–1782 BC)

Dynasty 12 (2060–1991 BC)
Amunemhet I
Senwosret I
Amunemhet II
Senwosret II

TABLE 1.1 ◆ (*continued*)

Senwosret III
Amunemhet III
Queen Sobeknofru
Dynasty 13 (1782–1650 BC)
Khendjer

SECOND INTERMEDIATE PERIOD: DYNASTIES 14–17 (1782–1570 BC)

Dynasty 14 (1650 BC)
Dynasty 15–16 (1663–1555 BC)
Hyksos Kings
Dynasty 17 (1663–1570 BC)
Sekhenenre Tao II
Kamose

THE NEW KINGDOM: DYNASTIES 18–20 (1570–1069 BC)

Dynasty 18 (1570–1293 BC)
Ahmose
Amunhotep I
Thutmose I
Thutmose II
Thutmose III
Hatshepsut
Amunhotep II
Thutmose IV
Amunhotep III
Amunhotep IV/Akhenaten
Smenkhkare
Tutankhamun
Ay
Horemheb
Dynasty 19 (1293–1185 BC)
Ramesses I
Seti I
Ramesses II
Merneptah
Amenmesse
Seti II
Siptah
Twosret
Dynasty 20 (1185–1070 BC)
Sethnakht
Ramesses III
Ramesses IV–Ramesses XI
Herihor

THIRD INTERMEDIATE PERIOD: DYNASTIES 21–25 (1069–525 BC)

Dynasty 21 (1069–945 BC)
Smendes
Psusennes I
Pinedjem I (Thebes)
Amenemope
Dynasty 22 (945–712 BC)
Shoshenq I
Osorkon I

TABLE 1.1 ◆ *(continued)*

Dynasties 23–24 (818–712 BC)
'Libyan' Kings

KUSHITE PERIOD: DYNASTY 25 (772–656 BC)

Piankhy (Piye)
Shabaka
Taharqa

LATE PERIOD: DYNASTIES 26–31 (656–332 BC)

Dynasty 27 (525–404 BC)
(First Persian Domination)
Cambyses
Darius I
Xerxes
Dynasty 28 (404–399 BC)
Dynasty 29 (399–380 BC)
Dynasty 30 (380–362 BC)
Nectanebo I
Nectanebo II
Dynasty 31 (342–332 BC)
(Second Persian Domination)

SAITE PERIOD: DYNASTY 26 (656–525 BC)

Psammethicus I
Necho
Psammethicus II
Apries
Ahmose III
Psammethicus III

PTOLEMAIC PERIOD (332–30 BC)

Ptolemy I–XII
Cleopatra VII

ROMAN PERIOD (30 BC–AD 323)

Augustus Caesar

BYZANTINE PERIOD (AD 323–642)

ARAB CONQUEST (AD 642)

Source: After Brewer, Douglas J. and Teeter, Emily, *Egypt and the Egyptians* (Cambridge University Press, 1999)

event that occurred in a given year (Fig. 1.1). Thus a year might be referred to as 'the year of smiting the Inw' or 'the year of the plentiful harvest of King so-and-so'. The kings in turn were arranged into 31 consecutive dynasties (Dynasty 32 postdates Manetho) – a chronology that has been used for Egyptian history ever since.

Unfortunately, no complete copy of Manetho's work has ever been found. The earliest reference to it is contained in the writings of the Jewish scholar Josephus, dating from the mid-first century AD, and other

FIGURE 1.1 ◆ *A series of royal years (rectangular boxes) from the Palermo Stone, a Dynasty 5 king list.*   *Source*: Photograph by D. J. Brewer

sources are even later, dating from the third to the ninth centuries AD. Although each of Manetho's dynasties roughly represents a ruling family, the different authors of these later works do not agree with one another on the periods of time Manetho assigned to each dynasty, nor is it clear if Manetho's work recognised that during periods of civil war several families ruled Egypt simultaneously. Consequently, it is impossible using only Manetho's history to string all the dynasties together and come up with an accurate chronology. Attempts have been made, but they are inaccurate for the early dynasties by as much as 2,500 years.

Additional ancient king lists discovered by archaeologists and Egyptologists have, however, offered refinements to Manetho's chronology, increasing its accuracy. In all, five king lists have been discovered, all more or less supporting Manetho's work. Using all the king lists, combined with historical data from scholarly research, Egyptologists have converted Manetho's system into a viable dating tool that is quite accurate – so accurate that it was used as one of the first tests for carbon-14 dating when that technique was still being developed.

Scholars attribute real (absolute) dates to these dynasties through references to astronomical events and correlations with the three calendars (two lunar, one solar) in use in Egyptian antiquity. Like other ancient peoples, the early Egyptians were careful observers of the heavens. They watched the brightest star, Sothis (Sirius), as it cycled through the sky and noted that its yearly reappearance on the eastern horizon after a period of absence presaged the Nile's annual flood. Not surprisingly, the Egyptians decided to make this celestial event a marker for their administrative year. Four mentions of the rising of Sothis, generally known as Sothic dates, are preserved in texts from the third to the first millennia BC;

BOX 1.2 ◆ Coming forth of Sothis

'A statement that you should know that the Coming Forth of Sothis will happen on month 4 of Peret, day 16. Let this be noted [by] the temple priesthood of Power-of-Senwosret-true-of-voice, of Anubis who is upon his mountain, and of Sobek; also cause this letter to be entered in the temple daybook.'

[After Parkinson 1991]

---

absolute chronologies are computed from the more numerous recordings of lunar dates and cross-checked mathematically with the Sothic dates. Differences in interpreting the various lunar and Sothic dates do lead to some discrepancies between chronologies, particularly for the earliest dynasties. Late period dates are almost completely fixed, but the initial dynasties' dates are based on average reign lengths and are therefore approximate. Recent work on radiocarbon dates from Egypt has, however, yielded results encouragingly close to dates computed in the manner described above.

Although studies of Egypt's Dynastic Period are greatly aided by the dynastic chronology, research on Egypt's beginnings, in the Prehistoric Period, must rely on other methods. Excavation, which is based on the geological law of superposition, is one of archaeology's most important dating techniques. The law of superposition, simply put, states that a level or layer of earth is older than those that overlay it (Fig. 1.2). That is, as you excavate deeper into the earth, you encounter older sediments and artefacts. With proper measurement of artefact location and record-keeping, a scholar can mark the passage of time by noting which artefact was recovered from what stratigraphic layer and thereby create a relative chronology, meaning that a sequence of artefacts can be ordered from most recent to oldest. However, this does not allow us to fix precise calendrical (absolute) dates to the objects.

Seriation typology, previously called sequence dating, is another common means of establishing relative dates (see Chapter 2 for an in-depth discussion of this technique and its development). This technique involves noting how artefacts, particularly pottery and stone tools, change through time (Fig. 1.3). These objects serve as clues to associated

FIGURE 1.2 ◆ *Stratigraphic sequence showing overlaying units at an excavation of an Early Dynastic Delta site. Note the thin light-coloured layers of ash.*

Source: Photograph by D. J. Brewer

time periods; advances in manufacturing techniques as well as changes in style and artistic decoration often allow these objects to be ordered in a relative sequence. As with excavation, seriation does not give us exact dates for the objects, but it does allow us to deduce where they fall in a sequence from earliest to latest.

For absolute dates archaeologists often have to turn to physics and chemistry laboratories, where carbon-14, thermoluminescence, potassium argon and other radiometric analyses can be conducted. The end results of these tests, which measure the amount of radioactivity in an archaeological sample, are a chronological date given in years BC or AD. The accuracy of the date depends on the technique, the laboratory, the quality of the archaeological sample and the method of calibrating the laboratory date to compensate for the age of the sample and the geographic area of origin.

Carbon-14 dating is one of the most frequently used dating techniques and one of the most poorly understood by the general public. Carbon-14 dating is based on the radioactive isotope carbon-14. All living organisms

FIGURE 1.3 ◆ *Evolution of stone tools, from a large Acheulean hand axe, to a later more refined hand axe, to a delicate Neolithic projectile point.*

Source: Courtesy of the Spurlock Museum, University of Illinois

contain carbon-12 and carbon-14 in known quantities. Over time, the unstable carbon-14 becomes carbon-12. The amount of carbon-14 remaining in a once-living sample is thus a measure of time since the organism's death. There is, however, a finite amount of carbon-14 in any organism, and thus the technique has a dating limit of about 50,000 years, beyond which too few radioactive carbon-14 elements remain to make an accurate count. (A new enrichment technique has pushed the carbon-14 dating ability to nearly 70,000 years.) For samples within the technique's range, the carbon-14 is measured, a statistical average is compiled and a date is offered.

When you read a date of 3000 ± 100 years BC, this indicates that a statistical procedure has been applied to the raw data, whereby, based on the mathematical laws of statistical probability, there is a 66 per cent chance that the date of the object in question falls within the period 3100–2900 BC. The older or poorer the sample is, the larger the error factor (i.e. ± a larger number). Because dates are based on statistical (parametric) averages and thus hold only a 66 per cent chance of being correct, it is important to retrieve more than one sample of a given strata or object for testing. The ideal is to retrieve samples in a stratigraphic sequence. Incorrect carbon-14 dates are common and only through a series of tested samples can dates be deemed fully reliable.

Another less common dating technique applied in Egypt is thermoluminescence, or TL dating. TL dating is based on the assumption that the clay and other particles used to make ceramic vessels hold naturally occurring radioactive elements. When the vessel is fired, these trapped elements are released from the clay. Through time, however, the hard-fired vessel's clay matrix recaptures radioactive elements, and when a sample of pottery is heated in the laboratory, the amount of these elements given off is a measure of the sample's age and can be converted into a chronometric date. Although thermoluminescence dating has been in use for about 40 years, it is not considered as reliable as carbon-14 dating, and calibrating the raw counts to an AD or BC date has yet to be defined as clearly as carbon-14 dating or the dynastic chronology.

Although other technologies exist for dating archaeological finds, those presented here constitute the most commonly used in Egypt. Clearly, explaining Egypt's history and prehistory is best served by close cooperation between historians, prehistorians, natural scientists, Egyptologists, archaeologists and other associated scholars. The picture of the past that these disciplines can bring to life depends on the cooperative assembling of facts derived from these very different scholarly pursuits. This picture is only recently coming into focus for the Predynastic Period.

Egyptologists and archaeologists undertake these tasks due to a fundamental human curiosity about our past. Many of the concerns of ancient life, such as the quality of the year's harvest, paying taxes, finding a spouse and raising safe and healthy children, mirror our modern ones. History holds important lessons. Many ancient civilisations collapsed because of exhausted natural resources, prolonged war and fast-moving disease – threats that face us still. As the Spanish poet and philosopher George Santayana so aptly phrased it, those who cannot remember the past are doomed to repeat it.

CHAPTER 2

· · · · · · · · · · · · · · ·

Archaeology and Egyptian prehistory

Scientific study of Egypt's ancient culture began in the mid-1600s when John Greaves of Oxford travelled to Egypt and made the first extensive study of the Giza pyramids. Unfortunately, other European expeditions of his day were not so informative, most providing nothing more than sketchy accounts and poor drawings of what was encountered. Napoleon's 1798 military campaign into Egypt, however, ushered in a new era of Egyptian enquiry. Napoleon commissioned a special scientific team of 150 scholars (geographers, geologists, naturalists and historians) to sojourn up the Nile under military guard and document all they encountered (Fig. 2.1). The trials and tribulations of these tremendously brave and dedicated savants make for fascinating reading, and their lasting legacy was *La Description de l'Egypte* (1809–1830), a massive 24-volume work covering Egypt's flora, fauna, anthropology and antiquities.

Napoleon's defeat and the subsequent cessation of hostilities, coupled with the publication of *La Description*, lured many more scholars to the Nile Valley, and 'Egyptomania' began to sweep across Europe. Not all who travelled to Egypt, however, were interested in uncovering its past for scientific purposes; many came to profit from the sale of its antiquities. To curb the wholesale looting of Egypt's past, strict regulations were finally placed on excavations, and overseen by a government office of 'Egyptian Antiquities'. From the mid-nineteenth century on, applications to excavate had to be submitted and the scientific value of the project evaluated before an excavation permit was issued.

FIGURE 2.1 ◆ *The Battle of the Pyramids. This 1806 painting captures the decisive engagement in July 1798 when French troops under Napoleon's command defeated Egypt's Mamaluke rulers, thereby allowing the accompanying scholars to begin their dangerous trek up the Nile.*

Source: Erich Lessing/Art Resource, NY, Musée des Beaux-Arts, Lille, France

Work on Egypt's prehistory and early historic past (*c*.5500–2613 BC) began in earnest in the late 1800s and in many ways parallels or in some instances is directly responsible for the birth of contemporary archaeology. The British archaeologist, Sir William Flinders Petrie (Fig. 2.2), the father of modern archaeology, is credited with many of the great discoveries of this period. Guy Brunton, Gertrude Caton-Thompson, Herman Junker, James Quibell, Jacques de Morgan and a host of others, many of whom were Petrie's students, made other important contributions. Competition among archaeologists from different nations was quite fierce in the nineteenth and early twentieth centuries, and the national politics of the day were reflected in the hunt for Egypt's prehistoric origins. French, German, British and later American archaeologists vied with one another for the honour of defining the origins of ancient Egypt,

FIGURE 2.2 ◆ *William F. Petrie at the height of his career (c.1900).*

a quest that continues to this day. Working without the aid of modern dating techniques, these early archaeologists defined a series of cultures that predate the now famous Pharaonic era of Egypt.

The remarkable and famously cantankerous Sir Flinders Petrie was the first to devise a rudimentary dating system, using the size, shape and artistic style of pottery and other artefacts. His work revealed a prehistoric world composed of complex cultures rich in diversity; cultures that ultimately led to the founding of Egypt's First Dynasty. Petrie was the first to define this prehistoric era as the 'Predynastic Period'. He does not, however, deserve all the credit for its discovery: he owed much of his success to a French competitor, Jacques de Morgan (Fig. 2.3).

Although Petrie worked out a detailed sequence of pottery expressing the passage of time through the Predynastic Period, he initially assigned the pottery to the First Intermediate Period, which dates more than 1,000 years later. Jacques de Morgan, while working at a different Predynastic site, recognised the pottery as actually predating everything that had been found up to that point. And it was de Morgan who later connected

BOX 2.1 ◆ Sir Flinders Petrie

Petrie, like many of the great scholars of his day, was considered a 'character'. He insisted on rigorous discipline in the field and maintained his staff on a Spartan diet of tinned food, which was often shared cold in the can. Tourists witnessed him neck-deep in filthy canals or surveying on the Giza plateau in his long underwear.

Petrie began his career in Egypt surveying the pyramids. At his father's urging he planned to verify the writings of family friend Piazzi Smyth, who believed great knowledge was held within the physical measurements of the pyramids. Unfortunately, Petrie found all the published measurements to be incorrect and with a grant from the Royal Society published his first work: *The Egyptian Pyramids*. Thereafter he signed on with the Egypt Exploration Society to conduct further fieldwork.

Although showing great prowess in mathematics he was admittedly poor at languages, even though his mother, who spoke several languages, tried to instil in him her talents. Still, it is amazing that he never mastered even the rudiments of colloquial Arabic, which more than once led to disaster. In one instance, after spending the better part of a day hauling a sarcophagus out of its resting-place, he yelled 'push' instead of 'pull', causing the artefact to tumble back into the tomb chamber, totally destroying it.

Personality quirks aside, it is fair to say that Petrie's contribution to archaeology did not end with his discoveries but was carried on by his students, who, engrained with his work ethic and influenced by his methods, made some of the most important discoveries of their day.

Petrie's pottery sequence to the pottery of the early dynasties. One can only imagine how Petrie felt when one of his rivals (and a Frenchman at that!) bested him by first recognising the existence of the Nile Valley's Predynastic cultures. According to Petrie, however, de Morgan 'proved' nothing – proof came by way of Petrie's sequence dating system.

Petrie's Predynastic cultural sequence was based on dating objects and sites by the type and style of artefacts recovered from excavation. Just

FIGURE 2.3 ◆ *Jacques de Morgan at about the time of his early Predynastic discoveries (c.1889).*

as one can assess an automobile's year of manufacture based on subtle changes in body style and other features, Petrie was able to separate time periods based on subtle changes in the appearance of artefacts' shape, decoration and method of manufacture. For example, by looking at the wavy handles of a series of large ceramic jars, he was able to track this style of jar through history (Plate 1). In its earliest manifestation, the vessel type had a functional handle in a wavy shape, but through time the wavy handle turned into a simple decorative motive. By association, other ceramic vessels could be dated and their styles monitored through time as well, eventually creating a body of artefact styles that indicated particular periods of time. Archaeologists working elsewhere in Egypt could then compare their artefacts with Petrie's system and date their sites.

Although Petrie's system of sequence dating, or seriation typology, has undergone considerable refinement, it is still a fundamental tool of modern archaeology, as are the terms he coined to define the general time periods and their corresponding cultures. Essentially the cultural periods of Egypt's late Prehistoric Period were named after the site where the first evidence was discovered (Table 2.1).

TABLE 2.1 ◆ *Predynastic sequence and its modern derivations*

Date (BC)	Upper Egypt	Lower Egypt
3150	Protodynastic	Protodynastic
3300	Naqada III	Naqada III
3400	Naqada IIcd (Late Gerzean)	Ma'adian (Late Gerzean)
3650	Naqada IIab (Early Gerzean)	Omari B (?)
3750	Naqada I (Amratian)	Omari A (?)
4400	Badarian	
4800		Merimden
5200		Fayyum A

Source: After Brewer, Douglas J. and Teeter, Emily, *Egypt and the Egyptians* (Cambridge University Press, 1999)

Petrie excavated at almost every major site in Egypt, and his work set the standard for scientific archaeological research. His meticulous excavations, thorough analysis and careful and immediate publication were unequalled by his contemporaries. Petrie made many significant contributions to the field of archaeology in general, but perhaps the most important was his insistence that everything recovered from an archaeological site was important, even pieces of broken pottery, bones, bricks, beads and worked flint. He believed that these artefacts, if analysed properly, could offer as much insight into ancient Egyptian culture as a horde of museum-quality vases or carved reliefs. Likewise, Petrie also encouraged excavating less glamorous sites such as small towns and houses, which, although they did not yield quality works of art, provided much material that elucidated the culture of ancient Egypt. He further contributed to Egyptian archaeology by training Egyptian field assistants known as Kuftis (villagers from the town of Kuft) and students who later went on to conduct their own research.

Petrie students such as Eric Peet and Guy Brunton and associates like Gertrude Caton-Thompson, as well as other archaeologists such as Herman Junker, Oswald Menghin and Ferdinan Debono, just to name a few, conducted excavations at various prehistoric sites in both Upper and Lower Egypt from the early 1900s to the 1950s. Through their work we can begin to trace the outlines of several prehistoric and Predynastic cultures from which regional chronologies were constructed.

An entirely new era of scholarship began in the 1960s, when the rising waters from the newly built Aswan High Dam threatened the Nubian monuments in southern Egypt and northern Sudan. To save

Box 2.2 ◆ Saving the Nubian monuments

The threat to Egypt's and the Sudan's cultural past through the construction of the Aswan High Dam brought together scholars from many fields and countries dedicated to saving Nubia's history. The protection of temples and monuments like those at Philae and Abu Simbel presented considerable technical and financial challenges. In the case of Abu Simbel, several projects were considered: the one finally chosen consisted of dismantling the temple by cutting it into huge blocks, removing them and rebuilding the temple higher on the cliff in a simulated environment. The project was successfully completed and the temple officially reopened in September 1968. Other Nubian monuments were also moved, but some were sacrificed to the rising waters of Lake Nasser.

the monuments, traditional Egyptologists as well as archaeologists versed in European and North American archaeology came to the Nile Valley to help with the preservation efforts. Perhaps for the first time since Napoleon's invasion, Egyptologists, archaeologists, prehistorians and natural scientists worked together towards a common goal. After the Nubian campaign was completed, many of these scholars continued to work in the Valley, addressing questions about Egypt's prehistoric and early historic past. Utilising modern technology such as carbon-14 dating, ground-penetrating radar, satellite reconnaissance, and scientific sampling procedures, as well as knowledge gained from other scientific disciplines such as geology and biology, archaeologists began to reveal a much more complete picture of the area's distant past (Plate 2).

Through controlled scientific excavations, modern archaeologists have been able to reconstruct a general progression of cultures through Egypt's prehistory. Thanks to carbon-14 dates, stone tool seriation (à la Petrie) and the reconstruction of past environments through the study of archaeologically recovered plant and animal remains, a picture, albeit vague, of Egypt's distant past is now available.

The vagueness of the prehistoric picture is due in part to the type of information that prehistorians recover, the vast blocks of time studied and the tools used to interpret the material finds. Unlike historians or Egyptologists who can view a literary work or sometimes even a piece of art and pinpoint its age to a given decade or year, prehistorians must analyse and interpret materials tens of thousands of years old that are more often than not poorly preserved and can only be roughly dated. With no written record to use for comparisons, prehistorians understandably must be cautious in making conclusions about the past.

Nevertheless, we now know that, as in other parts of the world, Egypt's prehistoric inhabitants lived a life dominated by hunting, fishing and gathering wild plants. The first Egyptians were probably *Homo erectus*, followed by the Neanderthals and later *Homo sapiens* (anatomically modern humans). Archaeologists have found that as early as 20,000 BC a variety of different cultures lived along the Nile and practised a way of life reminiscent of later Egyptian peoples. With the onset of sedentary living and the introduction of domestic plants and animals (c.6000 BC), a direct sequence of progressively more complex cultures (the Predynastic) led to the coronation of Egypt's first kings.

According to Egyptian priests, who told their stories to ancient Greek and Roman travellers, from these prehistoric antecedents two kingdoms eventually evolved: one in southern Egypt and one in the Nile Delta. Tradition holds that these separate kingdoms were unified about 3050 BC by Menes, a chieftain-king from southern Egypt, who conquered the Delta through military might. But is this legend of unification true? Modern archaeological research suggests that unification was a much more complicated affair than the legend suggests, involving many individuals, most of whom remain mysterious figures of the past.

Nevertheless, from this time on the Nile Valley from Aswan to the Mediterranean was ruled by a line of hereditary kings who surrounded themselves with elaborate ritual that celebrated their office and person. From existing, albeit meagre, textual evidence, we know that by the time of the reign of Den, Egypt's fourth (Dynasty I) king (c.2890 BC), two enduring symbols of the unity of the Two Lands had appeared: the double crown (a headdress that combined the red crown of the north with the white crown of the south) and the title *nsw bity* (literally, 'he of the reed and bee'), both of which signify the holder as king of a united Egypt.

After 360 years of unified rule by seven kings, the basic fabric of Egyptian culture that was to endure for the next 3,000 years had become established. By the beginning of the Third Dynasty (c.2686 BC), society had become heavily stratified and the state strongly centralised, ruled from the capital city of Memphis. The country was headed by a semi-divine king who was assisted by a highly articulated bureaucracy led by a prime minister (*chaty* or vizier). The country was divided into a series of districts, each overseen by a governor who was directly responsible to the prime minister (Table 2.2). Although the royal family filled many administrative positions, the deliberate moving of officials from one post to another appears to have been an effort to forestall true hereditary passage of offices. Egypt during this period was touted as an upwardly mobile society, with those born to humble circumstances able to rise to powerful positions through skill and eloquence.

The vast majority of the evidence for this formative era is derived from analysing archaeological remains such as pottery, sculpture, tools, architecture and other byproducts of ancient daily life. These artefacts represent material expressions of activities, beliefs and ideas that can be interpreted by modern scholars.

TABLE 2.2 ◆ *Governing hierarchy of Early Dynastic Egypt.*

```
                              The King
                                 |
                             The Vizier
                                 |
        ┌────────────────────────┼────────────────────────────────┐
Royal Palace and Activities   Treasury              Regional Government
       ╱      ╲                    |                        |
Administrators  Overseer      Chancellor        ┌───────────┼───────────┐
and Controllers Royal Works        |        Upper       Lower        Oasis
       |           |         Taxation — Collection  Egypt   Egypt          |
    Palace      Ceremony          |           |      Nome        Nome      Desert
   Overseer     Overseer    Manufacturing  Storage  Governor   Governor  Administrator
                                   ╲       ╱           |           |
                              Redistribution        Town        Town
                                                    Mayors      Mayors
```

Source: After Wilkinson, Toby A. H., *Early Dynastic Egypt* (Routledge, 1999). Courtesy of Thompson Publishing Services

FIGURE 2.4 ◆ *The Step Pyramid of Saqqara.*   *Source*: Photograph by D. J. Brewer

Although a few texts from the Predynastic and Early Dynastic Periods (Dynasties 1–3) exist, they remain difficult to decipher because the rules of Egyptian grammar and spelling had not yet become fully codified, thereby creating confusion and ambiguity for modern translators. The information that has been gleaned from the early written records comes predominantly from lists of kings compiled at several different times in Egypt's history. As we saw in Chapter 1, several lists exist, most written several thousand years after the Predynastic and Early Dynastic Periods, but one list does date to the Pyramid Age (Dynasty 5), and all the lists name kings and events of the earliest dynasties. Two lists, the Palermo Stone and the Turin List (on papyrus), extend back into the Predynastic Period.

The best evidence of the early kings' tremendous power and the newly centralised government's efficiency is the first pyramids. The earliest of these great monuments is the Third Dynasty Step Pyramid at Saqqara, one of the earliest examples of massive stone architecture in the world. The sheer size of this monument and the means by which it was constructed are important indicators of the power and organisation that had evolved in Egypt by the end of its formative era (Fig. 2.4).

CHAPTER 3

· · · · · · · · · · · · · · · ·

Environmental reflections

Daily life in ancient Egypt was so intertwined with the environment that many aspects of this ancient civilisation are barely intelligible without reference to its natural surroundings. The rhythms of nature – the cycle of the sun, the rise and fall of the Nile, the seasonal agricultural cycles – are reflected throughout ancient Egyptian culture. For instance, the local fauna and flora were incorporated as signs in hieroglyphic writing, floral motifs were used to adorn the tops of columns and many day-to-day objects were fashioned in the form of animals. Even the great pylon gateways standing at the entrance to temples were symbolic representations of the mountains and plateaux that run adjacent to the Nile (Fig. 3.1).

Egypt is a land of environmental contrasts. In its vast deserts the Earth's surface is subjected to intense heat, aridity and wind. Under these harsh conditions the landscape remains barren, and shifting sands cover roads and landmarks, making navigation difficult. Today, Egypt is almost rainless. The average annual rainfall for the entire country is only about 10 mm (0.39 in.), with most of it falling along the Mediterranean coast. In some parts of Egypt several years may pass between rains, and some of the highest recorded temperatures on Earth have come from these areas (Fig. 3.2). Through this vast, arid wilderness flows the Nile River, creating an ecosystem that defined Egyptian culture (Plate 3).

From its source in Uganda to its mouth in the Mediterranean Sea, today's Nile runs more than 6,625 km (4116.7 miles) and is the longest river in the world (Fig. 3.3). The river flows virtually due north: its source and its mouth lie within one degree of the same meridian of longitude

FIGURE 3.1 ✦ *Natural motifs in day-to-day Egyptian objects: (a) hieroglyphs; (b) floral columns; (c) temple pylon entrance.*

Sources: (a) Erich Lessing/Art Resource, NY. Oriental Institute, University of Chicago; (b) Erich Lessing/Art Resource, NY. Saqqara Egypt; (c) Photograph by D. J. Brewer

FIGURE 3.2 ◆ *The Western Desert.*   *Source*: Photograph by D. J. Brewer

---

BOX 3.1 ◆ **Desert temperatures**

When the author was conducting archaeological research in the desert
near the Fayyum, ground temperature in the month of July reached
55°C (130°F) by 10:00 a.m. We could not determine the day's peak temperature, because our thermometer did not go beyond the 130° mark.
We were not able to measure ambient air temperature, which would
probably have been lower, because no one was willing to stand in the
sun all day holding a thermometer the required 2–3 metres (6–8 ft)
above the sand.

(31°E). Most of the modern Nile's water flows from two distinct sources.
Eighty-three per cent of its water comes from Lake Tana, high in the
Ethiopian plateau. Once a year, during the summer, monsoons fill the
lake and send water and silt down the Blue Nile, which causes the annual
inundation of Egypt, depositing rich agricultural silts along the Nile Valley.
The White Nile, which begins in Uganda, is the second main contributor
of water to the Egyptian Nile. The White Nile provides a much smaller

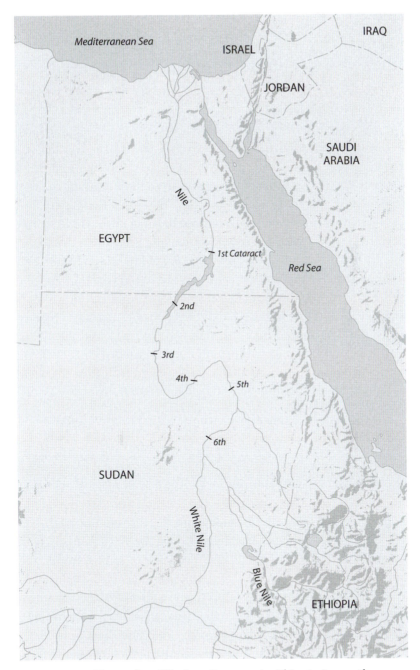

FIGURE 3.3 ◆ *The modern Nile from its source in Africa to its mouth.*

Source: Redrawn by Brenda Coelho

amount of water than the Blue Nile (approximately 16 per cent), but the source is steady. Without the water from the White Nile, the Egyptian Nile would probably run dry each May or June. The Blue and White Nile meet at the modern city of Khartoum in the Sudan. The River Atbara, also in the Sudan, is a third water source but provides less than 1 per cent of the Egyptian Nile's water.

The northerly flow of the Nile served as a natural compass for the ancient Egyptians, who thought of travel in terms of movement along the river. When Egyptians travelled to other lands, they noticed that the rivers ran the 'wrong' way, that is, north to south. For example, a New Kingdom text, dated to about 1530 BC, describes the Euphrates as 'the inverted water that goes downstream in going upstream'. The Nile's northerly flow also serves as a basis for modern geographic terminology. Southern Egypt, because it is upstream, is referred to as Upper Egypt, while the Delta in the north is known as Lower Egypt. During ancient times, Egypt was divided into four main geographic areas formed by the imaginary intersection of the river and the east–west passage of the sun. That is, the river flowed from the Valley to the Delta, and the sun rose over the Eastern Desert and set behind the Western Desert. Each of these geographic regions possessed unique physical and ecological characteristics, and each influenced the local inhabitants in different ways.

The Delta

The Delta, which represents 63 per cent of Egypt's inhabited area, is a flat and almost featureless plain (Fig. 3.4). It probably reached its modern dimensions by about 4000 BC. Today the Nile flows through the Delta via two principal branches, the Damietta and the Rosetta, but in antiquity there were three principal channels, known by the Egyptians as the 'water of Pre', 'the water of Ptah' and 'the water of Amun'. Today, these branches are known by their Greek and Roman names: the Pelusiac, the Sebennytic and the Canopic, respectively. Other branches mentioned by classical writers such as Herodotus were subsidiary branches of the 'water of Ptah' (e.g. the Mendesian and Saitic branches) or artificially cut channels (e.g. the Bolbitine and Bucolic). The Delta's Mediterranean coast is an extensive marshy area, interspersed with a series of lagoons and lakes, some of which are connected to the sea.

FIGURE 3.4 ◆ *The flat, almost featureless plain of the Nile Delta.*

Source: Photograph by Patrick Richard Carstens

To the casual observer, the Delta's only noticeable topographic features are *geziras*, deposits of sand, sandy clay and sandy silt that rise 1–12 metres (39.4 ft) above the surrounding cultivated fields (Fig. 3.5). While the origin of *geziras* is debated (they may represent relics of old buried branches of the Nile or be windblown, sand dune-like deposits), they are important archaeologically because they were ideal sites for prehistoric and Early Dynastic settlements. Villages and cemeteries built on the sterile *geziras* were safe from normal floods, and the surrounding fertile land was ideal for agriculture. The earliest habitation sites in the Delta are located on these *geziras*, a settlement pattern that is echoed in the ancient Egyptian belief that all life began on a mound of earth that emerged from primordial waters.

The Valley

Along most of its course through Egypt, the Nile has scoured a deep, wide gorge in the desert plateau and deposited a thick layer of rich, dark silt on the Valley floor – a deep carpet of silt that gives the Valley its astonishing

FIGURE 3.5 ◆ *Modern villages, like ancient ones, are often situated atop delta geziras. The distant village rising above the lowlands is situated on an ancient gezira* (see arrow). *Source*: Photograph by Patrick Richard Carstens

fertility. The annual floodwaters also added nutrients to the land and helped to curtail the build-up of salts (Plates 4 and 29).

At Aswan, near Egypt's ancient southern border, the Nile passes through a formation of hard igneous rock, which is more resistant to erosion than the softer sand and limestone found downstream, and this has resulted in a series of rapids called cataracts, forming a natural boundary to the south (Plate 5).

North of the first cataract at Aswan, where the Nile is deeper and the surface water smoother, igneous rocks are still obstacles and they form sand- and silt-covered islands. Cliffs border both sides of the Valley, but those on the west bank rapidly lose height to the north. Downstream (north) from Aswan the Nile flows in a northerly direction for about 200 km (124.2 miles) to the town of Armant before taking an acute 90° western bend, known as the Qena Bend. The Qena Bend extends for approximately 180 km (111.8 miles) and constitutes the river's only real divergence from a straight northerly flow. Along this bend, which separates the relatively narrow southern Valley from the wider Valley to the north, archaeologists have uncovered evidence for some the earliest Predynastic cultures. From Luxor to Cairo the Nile flows sinuously, and the flood plain is nearly 20 km (12.4 miles) wide in some places.

In antiquity, the Nile Valley was called *Kemet*, 'the Black Land', in reference to the rich agricultural plain. It was conceived of as composed of two parts: *Ta-mehu*, the north (from the Fayyum to the Mediterranean), and *Ta-shemaw*, the south (from Aswan to perhaps the Fayyum). Although the Egyptians considered the desert oases, at least politically, as part of Egypt, these peripheral areas did not enter into the conceptual sense of what was Egypt – the duality or balance formed by the Delta and Valley.

Oases and deserts

Egypt's deserts stood in stark contrast to the Nile Valley. The mountainous Eastern Desert (Fig. 3.6) and the Western sand desert (Fig. 3.7) were collectively referred to as *Djseret*, 'the Red Land', in contrast to *Kemet* or the Nile Valley proper.

The major oases of the Western Desert – Fayyum, Kharga, Dakhla, Bahiriya and Siwa – were considered Egypt's frontier outposts and served as military garrisons and stopping points along the caravan routes that connected the Nile Valley with the deserts and with sub-Saharan Africa. One of these caravan routes, still in use today, is the Darb el-Arbayin, the 'road of 40 [days]' that runs from Darfur in Sudan to Asyut.

One important oasis that stood in contrast to the others was the Fayyum, whose waters were connected to the Nile via the Bahr Yusef canal. It is the site of some of the earliest evidence for agriculture and later became one of the most agriculturally productive areas of Egypt. By New Kingdom times, population densities in the Fayyum were actually higher than in the Nile Valley proper. With its rich vineyards and planta-tions of flowers and fruit trees, the area is still one of the most agricultur-ally productive areas in modern Egypt.

The Nile in historical context

Egypt's climate has fluctuated through time, with resulting floral and faunal changes in the Nile Valley and desert. Beginning about 500,000

FIGURE 3.6 ◆ *(a) The mountainous Eastern Desert as seen from the Red Sea; (b) Bedouin moving through the difficult terrain of the Eastern Desert.*

Source: Photographs by D. J. Brewer

FIGURE 3.7 ◆ *The Western Desert near the Fayyum. The small structure in the foreground was the author's home for nearly a year while conducting research in the area.* Source: Photograph by D. J. Brewer

---

BOX 3.2 ◆ The Fayyum

At the turn of the twentieth century the Fayyum was not only agriculturally productive, but a sportsman's paradise as well. Fishing and hunting waterfowl were popular activities and could surpass any of the popular destinations of today's wealthy patrons of the sport(s). Nile perch in excess of 100 kg (220 lb) were not uncommon and ducks, in the thousands, visited the lake annually. The Aswan High Dam changed all this – the lake, no longer replenished by the annual Nile flood, began to shrink and became too saline to support the natural fauna. By the 1980s, the lake had become so salty that Mediterranean species were introduced and did, in fact, thrive for some time; a bucket full of shrimp or mullets could be purchased for a pittance. Sadly, today the lake is dead, the only form of life being a frog that is able to withstand the ultra saline conditions of the water.

years ago and lasting to around 125,000 years ago, Egypt received more rain than today, and many areas of the desert probably resembled modern African savannas. Following a brief period of hyper-aridity around 90,000 BC, moist conditions returned until 50,000 BC. Rainfall amounts then began to diminish gradually until the environment became similar to today's arid one around 30,000 BC. The beginning of the modern Nile River's course in approximately 10,000 BC coincided with a short-lived rainy interval and a return to savanna-like conditions throughout many parts of the Western Desert. During this time, evidence from rock art shows that giraffes, gazelle and ostriches roamed the area. From this time on, although minor fluctuations in precipitation occurred, Egypt became increasingly hot and dry, until the country's current climatic pattern became established during the Early Dynastic Period (c.3100–2700 BC) (Fig. 3.8).

Many introductory texts about Egypt label the Nile Valley's pre-historic environment as thoroughly inhospitable to humans, describing the Upper Egyptian Valley as a tangled jungle and the Delta as an uninhabit-able swamp. Modern research has disproved both of these characterisa-tions. For example, the Delta, although marshy in places, had numerous elevated *geziras*, and from very early times the central and southern Delta possessed considerable dry land suitable for habitation. Upper Egypt was always a well-drained flood plain able to support hunters and fishers in the Paleolithic Period and agriculturists in the Neolithic and Dynastic Periods.

The Nile's special character, which made it so central to Egyptian culture, was its annual inundation. Each June, the Nile began to rise

---

BOX 3.3 ◆ The Nile flood

The Nile flood is now controlled by two dams, the Aswan High Dam and the older Aswan Dam, which regulate water flow throughout the year. During the summer the water level of the river is quite high, to accommodate irrigation needs, and slowly falls throughout the winter. In early spring it reaches its lowest point; so low that houseboats along the Nile (the preferred living accommodation for archaeologists) lose power due to stretched and breaking electric lines.

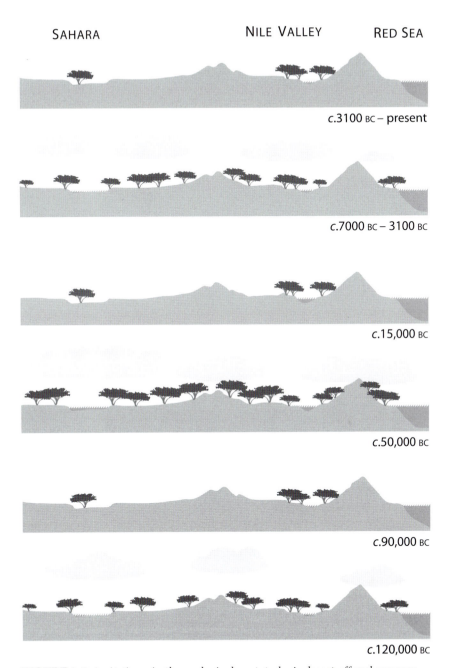

FIGURE 3.8 ◆ *At times in the geological past, today's desert offered savanna-like conditions and was inhabited by numerous cultures.*

Source: Redrawn by Brenda Coelho, after Hoffman 1984, Fig. 5

between Cairo and Aswan and the water turned green (a result of the brief efflorescence of myriad minute organisms). In August, the river rose rapidly and its waters turned muddy red from the rich red earth brought by the Blue Nile and the Atbara River. The Nile continued to rise until mid-September, then remained high for two or three weeks. In October, the river rose again slightly and then began to fall gradually until May, when the river reached its lowest level. If the Nile's floods were not controlled today by a series of dams, the cycle of inundation would be approximately the same as it was in historic times.

The Nile and its annual flooding created a convex flood plain, a topography typified by relatively high natural levees adjacent to the river tapering off to the more distant lowland areas approaching the desert border (Fig. 3.9). When the Nile flooded, the water passed through channels in the levees and covered most of the low-lying land up to the edge of the desert. When the floods subsided, the waters were trapped behind the levees in natural basins and could be used where they stood or channelled to other areas as dictated by agricultural needs. Today, the dams have made the basins obsolete for irrigation purposes, and these once-major features have been obscured by years of agricultural activity. Nevertheless, 130 basins have been identified ranging in size from ponds to small lakes. In ancient times they would have attracted breeding fish, birds and seasonal vegetation, offering a vastly different prospect from the well-drained valley we see today.

The ancient Egyptians fully understood the extent to which their lives and prosperity depended on the regularity of the inundation: a flood of 6 metres (19.7 ft) was perilously low and could result in shortages of food, while one of 9 metres (29.5 ft) could cause damage to crops and villages. The ancient Egyptians, therefore, never regarded the Nile and its gifts with complacency. Only by venerating the gods associated with the Aswan area (Khnum, Anukis and Satis) did they believe they might ensure a sufficient inundation. The so-called 'Famine Stela', a Late Period text carved on rocks at Sehêl near the First Cataract (Fig 3.10), relays how a famine was averted (supposedly) by King Djoser of Dynasty 3, who made donations of land and goods to the Temple of Khnum near Aswan.

Compared with the other great rivers of the world, the Nile's generally predictable floods provided dependable and abundant crop yields. The resulting surplus freed a significant segment of the population from

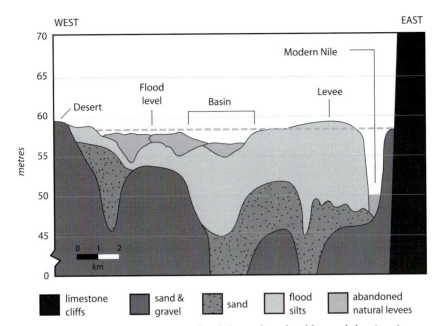

FIGURE 3.9 ◆ *The Nile's convex floodplain where land beyond the river is lower in elevation than the natural levees along the river's banks. When the annual floodwaters receded, the lowlands and basins served as natural reservoirs.* Source: After Brewer, Douglas J. and Teeter, Emily, *Egypt and the Egyptians* (Cambridge University Press, 1999). Redrawn by Brenda Coelho

agricultural labour, which allowed for the development of non-farming occupations such as full-time craftsmen, bureaucrats and priests. Although rivers like the Euphrates provided similar opportunities for crop surpluses and labour diversity, their unpredictability fostered a more pessimistic outlook on life and the hereafter. For example, Mesopotamians were never confident about the future. Because of their river's unpredictability, they felt that famine and other catastrophes were sure to happen sooner or later. In contrast, Egyptians held a more positive view of the future, looking forward to bettering themselves in this life as well as to a familiar and happy afterlife.

The Nile River also served as Egypt's principal highway. Because most villages were situated near the Nile, there was little incentive to develop land-based transport. Travel on the Nile was easy, facilitated by both the current (flowing northward) and the prevailing winds (blowing southward). Travel by means of the river was so common in ancient

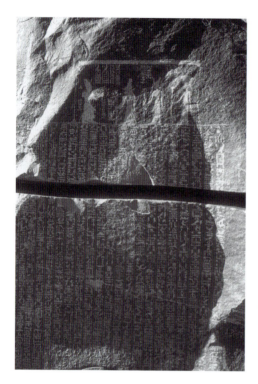

FIGURE 3.10 ◆ *The Famine Stela, reputedly erected by King Djoser, commemorates his successful attempt at averting an agricultural disaster by coaxing the Nile to flood so that Egypt's fields could be irrigated.*

Source: Photograph by Patrick Richard Carstens

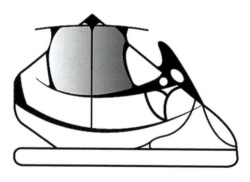

FIGURE 3.11 ◆ *The hieroglyph for 'to go south' – a boat with sail unfurled.*

Source: Redrawn by Carolynn Govoni

Egypt that the words for 'go south' and 'go north' were indicated in hieroglyphic script by boats with sail unfurled (upstream, with the prevailing wind) and boats with no sail (downstream, with the current), respectively (Fig. 3.11).

The river offered both an obvious means of mass transit and an easy way to move goods. During the annual inundation, when most of the

BOX 3.4 ◆ **River travel**

Contemporary travel in Egypt still relies heavily on the Nile. In an
archaeology expedition to el-Hibeh, the author often had to transport
goods in a type of sailboat called a *felucca*. As in ancient times, the current aids downstream transport and the prevailing winds aid upstream
travel, but not every night are the winds strong enough to accommodate
a heavily laden sailboat. One evening, it took many hours to traverse
the Nile, from west bank to east bank, causing great anxiety among our
village hosts when darkness fell and we had not yet returned. Thinking
we may have been kidnapped, they met our *felucca* heavily armed, just
in case persuasion was needed to secure our release. Needless to say,
our boat fare was minimal for that trip.

cultivated area was covered by water, barges could convey heavy cargo.
For example, building stones could be shipped directly from the quarries
situated in the cliffs bordering the flooded Valley to their destinations
at the cemeteries located just beyond the limits of the floodwaters.
Even after the introduction of wheeled vehicles during the Second Intermediate Period (1782–1570 BC), boats remained the dominant means of
transportation for people and goods.

The strong contrasts of the natural environment, which ancient
Egyptians witnessed on a daily basis, laid the foundation for their cultural identity and perception of the world. Their view of life was similar
to the world in which they lived: a world composed of opposites, with no
middle ground. A proper balance was needed for life to function in an
orderly manner, and this balance was composed of equally weighted
pairs: good and evil, light and dark, Upper Egypt and Lower Egypt, red
land and black land. The ability to stand, literally, with one foot on the
rich black soil of the Valley and one foot on the barren desert is but one
example of nature reinforcing the clarity of opposites so embedded in the
Egyptian psyche (Plate 6). Egyptians of the Late Prehistoric and Early
Dynastic Periods were industrious, optimistic, confident – and very xeno-
phobic. Their mind-set served them well, carrying them through nearly
3,000 years of recorded history and several thousand years of prehistory.

CHAPTER 4

· · · · · · · · · · · · · · ·

The Paleolithic:
A desert in bloom

The Paleolithic (literally 'Old Stone Age') represents the earliest period of human activity in Egypt. The term is used by archaeologists the world over to refer to the period prior to agriculture when stone was the dominant raw material for tool-making. Although bone and wood tools were made by Paleolithic peoples as well, poor preservation has left us few examples of these implements. In Egypt, as elsewhere, the Paleolithic is divided into three main periods: Lower, Middle and Upper, each with a set of characteristic tool types used to date archaeological sites (Table 4.1).

Paleolithic sites in Egypt are generally found near sources of water, such as the Nile or ancient oases, or where raw materials for making tools abound, such as on eroded hilltops (Figs 4.1 and 4.2). The earliest tools known from the Nile Valley date to about 300,000 years ago and come from the cliffs across the Nile from Abu Simbel. The earliest Paleolithic sites in Egypt's deserts date from roughly 250,000–90,000 BC.

Egypt's Paleolithic sites are typically quite eroded, and artefacts are sparse. The Umm Shagir site (see Fig. 4.3), a good example, sits on top of a 150-metre (492 ft) hill and consists of a scatter of 159 artefacts spread over a half kilometre of territory – hardly a rich site in comparison with Early Dynastic sites which frequently yield 500 or more artefacts in a single square metre. Fortunately, not all Lower Paleolithic sites produce so few artefacts. Arkin 8, for example, produced 3,407 artefacts in a 40 by 80 square metre area (only one-eighth of the entire site) and the site also provided evidence of an early structure thought to date to about 100,000 BC.

TABLE 4.1 ◆ *Upper, Middle and Lower Paleolithic industries of Egypt.*

Date	Period	Egyptian variant
5000 BC	Neolithic	
		Qarunian
		Shamarkian
6500 BC	Epi-paleolithic	
		Arkinians
		Qadan
		Halfan
		Kubbaniyan
		Idfuan
20,000 BC	Upper Paleolithic	
		Khormusan
		Aterian
		Mousterian
90,000 BC	Middle Paleolithic	
		Arkin 8
		Umm Shagir
		Bir Sahara 14
300,000 BC	Lower Paleolithic	

FIGURE 4.1 ◆ *An extinct oasis of the Western Desert. The parallel ridges reflect the ancient shoreline of a small lake. When active, this lake hosted an abundance of waterfowl, local game animals, vegetation and Paleolithic peoples.* *Source*: Photograph by D. J. Brewer

FIGURE 4.2 ◆ *The small mounds (inselburgs) represent more erosion-resistant sediments, which harbour an abundance of flint nodules ideal for stone tool making.* *Source*: Photograph by D. J. Brewer

This structure, composed of a series of sandstone blocks arranged in a semi-circle with a 1.8 metre by 1.2 metre (5.91 ft by 3.94 ft) oval-shaped foundation dug some 30 cm deep, probably represents a temporary or seasonal residence. If this structure is indeed a house, it is one of the earliest constructed dwellings in the world.

Another Lower Paleolithic site located deep in the desert is Bir Sahara 14, which lies around an ancient spring (Fig. 4.3). Its early date (*c*.100,000+ BC) as well as the association of stone tools with ostrich eggshell and animal bones makes it, along with Arkin 8, one of the most important Lower Paleolithic sites in Egypt.

One hundred thousand years ago, when Arkin 8 and Bir Sahara 14 were occupied, the river flowing through Egypt was the Protonile. It had numerous intertwined (braided) channels rather than a single channel like the modern Nile, and Egypt's deserts looked more like the Serengeti Plain than the vast desolate regions of today. Giraffes, gazelle and even elephants roamed the land, and hippopotami were quite common in and along the river.

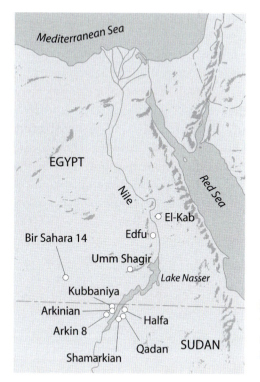

FIGURE 4.3 ◆

The approximate site location of the Paleolithic cultures discussed in the text.

Source: Redrawn by Brenda Coelho

A moister, rainier period prevailed from 120,000–90,000 BC, enabling Lower Paleolithic people to live and hunt on these ancient savannas. These were not lush grasslands, but rather seasonal savannas marked by an annual moist period. Because waterholes were sparse and separated by vast areas of arid land, migration out on to the savannas most probably occurred during the rainy season. During the dry season the area's inhabitants would have retreated to oases and other permanent sources of water.

Although Lower Paleolithic sites like Bir Sahara 14 and Arkin 8 do reveal important information about Egypt's earliest inhabitants, they cannot be precisely dated because they extend beyond the 50,000–70,000-year limit of the carbon-14 dating method. Furthermore, because they are surface sites, we cannot date them using geology. Thus we can offer only approximate dates based on the style and sophistication of the stone tools, which has led to some confusion in ordering these early sites and to many scholarly debates over their dates. Fortunately, more precise dating does not pose such a problem for numerous later sites.

About 90,000 years ago, the rains that characterised the Lower Paleolithic Period were interrupted, and for a short time the Sahara became a vast hyper-arid desert. During this dry spell, the peoples inhabiting these lands took refuge in the Nile Valley and the great oases, such as Kharga. Soon, a more humid climate returned, and scientists call this the Middle Paleolithic. Springs, lakes and lush grasslands covered much of the Sahara, surpassing the savanna conditions that had prevailed in the earlier Lower Paleolithic Period. At about this time, the inhabitants of Egypt and northern Africa (called the Mousterians) developed a more efficient way to make stone tools. This new technique, by which the flakes rather the stone core become the tools, is called Levalloisian after the site in France where this type of artefact was first discovered (Fig. 4.4 and Box 4.1). Perhaps most important among the new tools manufactured by the Levallois process was the stone projectile point, which enabled Middle Paleolithic people to become more efficient hunters, to seek larger and different kinds of game and to pursue that game across all of North Africa.

Whether technological innovation and the onset of a more hospitable climate were coincidental or connected is not certain, but thanks to these factors (and also others we will probably never know) a true flowering of Paleolithic cultures occurred at that time. In fact, some areas of the desert are literally carpeted with Middle Paleolithic tools (Fig. 4.5).

BOX 4.1 ◆ Levallois technique

Simply put, Acheulean tools were made by chipping flakes off a stone, the remaining stone core becoming the tool (Fig. 4.4a, c). In the later Levallois technique, the stone core (Fig. 4.4b) provided the raw material and the flakes became the tool (Fig. 4.4d), with many tools made from one stone. Because the core was specially prepared for flaking, each flake could be made thin and symmetrical, which meant more and different types of tools could be made from a single stone than using the previous Acheulean technique.

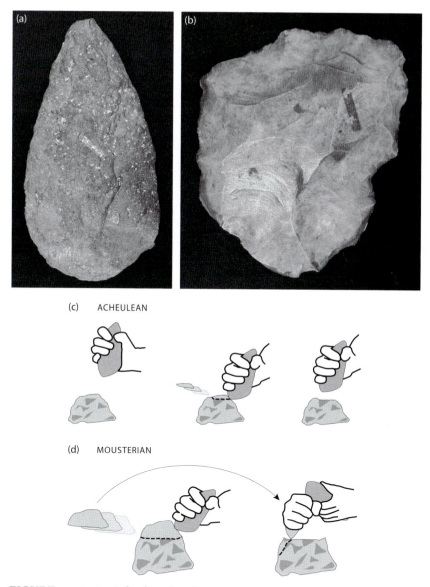

FIGURE 4.4 ◆ *An Acheulean hand axe (a, c) and a Mousterian core (b) from which flakes were created (d) to make the smaller more refined tools of the Levallois technique (see Box 4.1).*

Sources: (a, b) Courtesy of the Spurlock Museum, University of Illinois;

(c, d) Redrawn by Loren Kirkwood

FIGURE 4.5 ◆ *A Mousterian site of the Western Desert.*

Source: © Copyright The British Museum

The Middle Paleolithic Aterian culture (Table 4.1), which flourished in Egypt from 40,000 to 30,000 BC, exemplifies the technical and cultural advances of the times. One of the Aterians' most characteristic tools was a finely flaked projectile point, which was probably affixed to a dart and hurled via a throwing stick (Fig. 4.6). This weapon was the big game rifle of its time, and the vast increase in number and type of bones recovered from Aterian sites is evidence of its effectiveness. The faunal remains reported from Aterian sites include a large extinct aurochsen (cow), two species of gazelle, antelopes of different sizes, wild ass, fox, jackal, warthog, ostrich, turtle and birds.

Interestingly, the Aterians, with their sophisticated tools and hunting prowess, lived side by side with other peoples who used simpler tools and lacked the finely made dart points. Some sites are separated by a mere 14 km (8.7 miles), suggesting that food was plentiful enough to allow different cultures to live amicably and successfully on the Saharan savannas during the Middle Paleolithic. At about the same time that Aterians and other Mousterian cultures were prevalent in the Western Desert, people referred to as Khormusans were living along the river. Like

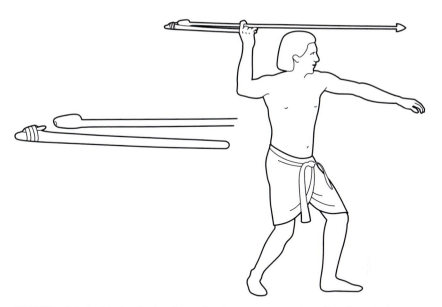

FIGURE 4.6 ◆ *Aterian technology: the dart, a stone point affixed to a light shaft, is propelled with greater force when aided by a specially designed throwing stick.*   *Source:* Redrawn by Loren Kirkwood

Aterians, Khormusans appear to have been hunters, but they were also adept fishers.

In an attempt to simplify the cultural landscape of Paleolithic Egypt, some scholars prefer to order these groups into a sequence from Mousterian to Aterian, culminating with the Khormusan. Radiocarbon dates suggest, however, that these groups overlapped for many thousands of years. Apparently, as long as the desert remained relatively hospitable, Mousterians, Aterians, Khormusans and probably many other groups prospered and lived side by side.

Beginning around 37,000 BC the climate began to dry up, and by 30,000 BC Egypt's environment was as arid as it is today. The flora and fauna of the Western Desert disappeared, and the Middle Paleolithic peoples living there lost their food sources. Even the great Kharga Oasis apparently disappeared and was abandoned for nearly 20,000 years.

What happened to the Aterian and Mousterian peoples? To be sure, many groups may have died out, but some are likely to have gravitated to the Nile. There they encountered people of the Khormusan culture and probably other groups that archaeologists have yet to discover. At that time the Nile Valley must have had sufficient vegetation and game to support the newcomers. Without efficient river transport, however, these groups were unable to establish and maintain regular contact with each other, so their cultural differences persisted and grew, giving rise to the numerous diverse cultural traditions of the Late Paleolithic.

Based on geological evidence such as Nile and desert sediments, as well as plant and animal fossils, prehistorians believe a moister, more hospitable climate returned to Egypt from about 17,000 to 13,000 BC. At this time a newly adapted river-oriented culture referred to as Halfan came to dominate a stretch of the Nile extending from the second cataract to Kom Ombo, an area of 360 km. The earliest Halfan sites possess Levallois tools, but later sites are characterised by highly specialised flake tools, called microliths, many less than 3 cm (1.2 in.) long (Fig. 4.7). These were created for use in compound tools like the bow and arrow or

FIGURE 4.7 ◆ *Microlithic tools of the Late Paleolithic.*

Source: Courtesy of the Spurlock Museum, University of Illinois

the harpoon, and are indicative of the final phase of the Paleolithic Period, the Upper (or Late) Paleolithic. Microliths represent a refinement over the earlier Khormusan technology, suggesting that Halfan people were better adapted to hunting and fishing along the Nile than their predecessors. We also have evidence that at least three other localised groups flourished in Upper Egypt between about 17,000 and 15,000 BC: the Kubbaniyan, the Idfuan and the Qadan.

Readers newly confronted with these many names for Egypt's ancient cultures may wonder why this terminology is necessary. In effect, these names serve the archaeological community much like the Latin taxonomic terms used in the biological sciences. When properly defined, these names offer a point of reference for scholars to identify materials and to compare new discoveries with previously published accounts.

A good example of the use of nomenclature can be seen in discussions of the Kubbaniyans. The Kubbaniyans, whose sites date to about 16,070–15,640 BC, used tiny microlithic tools and divided their time between two distinct but overlapping habitats. During the winter and spring (November to June), they camped on the borderlands between the dune fields and the floodplain of the Nile – a position that enabled them to exploit both the riverine fish and game and any grazing animals that might range into the hinterlands after a rare winter shower. When the Nile floodplain's annual inundation began in late June, the Kubbaniyans retreated farther back into the dunes to avoid the floodwaters. There they camped and exploited the fish trapped in pools left by the receding flood and hunted any game animals that fed or sheltered in the mini-oases created by the pooled flood water (Fig. 4.8). Along with evidence of the diverse menu they enjoyed, we find that the Kubbaniyans were storing food in addition to consuming it immediately. On the basis of the size and amount stored, Kubbaniyans apparently began to share with a larger social group than the immediate family. This change in material culture implies a larger social and ideological change, and demonstrates the Kubbaniyans' ability to assess 'quantities and duration' for stored foods.

Thanks to good published reports of Kubbaniyan sites and tools, archaeologists can distinguish them from other contemporary groups such as the Idfuans, who lived along the Nile in Upper Egypt (c.15,850–15,000 BC) and apparently practised the older, essentially more Middle Paleolithic way of life. The absence of microlithic tools in Idfuan sites

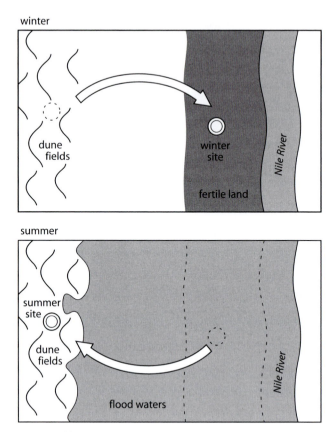

FIGURE 4.8 ◆ *Kubbaniyans moved seasonally between the border area of the Nile's fertile black soil and the desert swales (small dunes).*

Source: Redrawn by Loren Kirkwood

suggests a less efficient adaptation to fishing and hunting fowl and, perhaps, a continued reliance on older methods of hunting, trapping and snaring.

With the Qadan culture (13,000–9000 BC), we are fortunate to possess evidence that for the first time allows us to satisfy our curiosity about what these people looked like. Archaeologists discovered three Qadan cemeteries in an area that is now under the waters of Lake Nasser. Cemetery sites are very important to archaeologists, not because of a morbid curiosity about the dead, but rather for the diverse types of information that we can obtain from the study of graves and skeletons. Skeletal remains give us information about physical stature, diet and the diseases

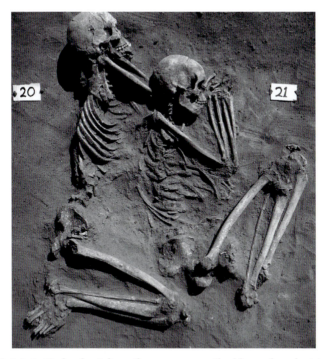

FIGURE 4.9 ♦ *Qadan burials as they were unearthed by archaeologists during the UNESCO-sponsored Nubian Monuments campaign.*

Source: © Copyright The British Museum

that plagued these early Egyptians. Analyses of the bones and graves can also provide important information about social class and religious beliefs, as well as longevity and quality of life.

A total of 59 skeletons of men, women and children were recovered from a Qadan cemetery (see Fig. 4.3), believed to be around 12,000 years old. The bodies were buried loosely flexed on their left sides with their heads to the east and facing south. More than one individual often shared the same grave (Fig. 4.9), and in general the bodies were buried in shallow oval pits covered by flat slabs of limestone. It is possible that small mounds of dirt once covered the graves but have long since eroded away. The Qadans show evidence of familiar physical ailments like arthritis, sacroiliac problems, osteitis and possibly spinal tuberculosis, as well as a variety of dental disorders, including missing teeth, cavities and abscesses.

Although the poor state of preservation and small number of individuals buried make it difficult to draw precise conclusions, burials from this one Qadan site revealed rather unexpected discoveries. First, the people buried there constitute what can be called a representative population: unlike most ancient cemeteries, which are usually dominated by the elderly and newborns, people of all ages were interred. A second unusual feature of the burials was the placement of 110 stone artefacts, almost all in positions that suggest they had penetrated the bodies as either arrow or spear points. Many of the artefacts were found along the vertebral column, but others were located in the chest cavity, lower abdomen, arms and skull. Indeed, several pieces were found still embedded in the sphenoid bones of the skull, in positions that indicate the projectiles had entered from under the lower jaw. In all, more than 40 per cent of the burials contained these small flake points. Four persons had suffered multiple wounds, with points still embedded in their bones. In the majority of cases, however, the points were not embedded in bone but lay within the skeletal remains, suggesting that they had penetrated the soft tissues. One grave yielded eight bodies that had apparently been buried together. Fractures on the arms and deep cut marks on the legs give further testimony to the violent nature of their deaths.

The obvious conclusion to be drawn from this evidence is that these Qadanians met a violent death – but why? What could have caused 40 per cent of the interred individuals to die violently? One possible reason could be conflict caused by a reduction in the food supply brought on by a return to arid conditions. With more people moving into the Nile Valley, equally affected by the loss of resources, territory might have become an issue, and the combination of limited food resources and increased territoriality might have sparked competition and eventually conflict between groups vying for the Nile Valley's most productive lands.

Finding the true reason behind the violent deaths of the Qadan people requires the ability to date the recovered skeletons precisely. For example, if these people were interred over a 150- or 200-year time span (the degree of error in any carbon-14 date of this age), then the number of deaths by violence would not be so dramatic. If, however, the bodies were interred as the result of a single episode or a series of repeated episodes over a short period of time, some specific issue or event clearly stimulated the violent interchange between peoples.

Interestingly, a Qadan cemetery located directly across t
dating to about the same time period revealed little evidence ᴏ₁ ._
Of the 39 skeletons recovered, only two showed any sign of violent
trauma. A few graves at a third cemetery near Tushka displayed the horns
of giant wild cattle (*Bos primigenious*) just above the interments, suggesting that at least some burials were marked in a manner seen in later Early
Dynastic royal graves, but again there is little evidence of violence. With
no precise date for these cemeteries and because they are now under the
waters of Lake Nasser, little opportunity remains for solving this mystery.

The final thousand years of the Upper Paleolithic Period in Egypt is
called the Epi-paleolithic. Epi-paleolithic tools were tiny, well-made
microliths; the small blades were often backed to prevent the user from
cutting his or her finger when working with the tool (Fig. 4.10). The Nile

FIGURE 4.10 ◆ *Epi-paleolithic 'backed' microblades. Note the delicately
flaked back (right side) of each blade, which has been worked to protect the user
from cutting his/her finger when applying downward pressure on the flint.*

Source: Courtesy of the Spurlock Museum, University of Illinois

Valley site of El-Kab reveals a full stratigraphic sequence of Epi-paleolithic life: the lowest Epi-paleolithic occupation level was carbon-14 dated to c.6400 BC, a middle level to 6040 BC and the upper level to 5980 BC. More than 4000 artefacts were recovered, most of which were tiny microlithic tools such as burins and minutely retouched blades. Ostrich eggshell beads were also common, indicating that people wore ornamentation. Because the sites have yielded many badly decayed fish bones and were located so close to the river that they could only have been occupied during the river's low water stages, they probably represented seasonal fishing sites.

The pattern of Epi-paleolithic life suggested at El-Kab is echoed in other areas of Egypt. For example, further to the south near the modern Egyptian border with Sudan, the Arkinians (8600 ± 150 BC) fished and hunted along the Nile. Their settlement consisted of a cluster of 13 oval debris concentrations, probably representing a seasonal camp used by a small group of individuals. Other groups, like the Shamarkian (c.5700 BC), located near the second cataract (see Fig. 4.3), also developed a Nile-oriented way of life.

One of the most intriguing mysteries of prehistoric Egypt is the transition from Paleolithic to Neolithic life, represented by the transformation from hunting and gathering to sedentary farming. We know very little about how and why this change occurred. Perhaps nowhere is this cultural transition more accessible than in the Fayyum depression. Not only was there a vibrant Epi-paleolithic tradition living along the shore of the lake, but some of the earliest Neolithic dates have been recovered here as well. But even here, the 'why' and 'how' of the transition from hunting and gathering to a sedentary agricultural way of life remain difficult to decipher.

Today the Fayyum and its lake, Birket Qarun, lie about 44 metres (144 ft) below sea level. The lake is extremely saline and essentially void of any indigenous animal life (Fig. 4.11). During the Epi-paleolithic, however, the lake was connected to the Nile by a natural channel that replenished its waters every year during the annual flood. Along the lake's shores and in the surrounding marshes, groups of people belonging to the Epipaleolithic Qarunian or Fayyum B culture thrived. The area was home to a variety of fish and waterfowl, and wild animals watered there as well. Qarunian sites, dating from about 6240 to 5480 BC, can be

FIGURE 4.11 ◆ *Fayyum's Birket Qarun as viewed from the southern shore.*

Source: Photograph by D. J. Brewer

found all along the old lake shoreline. These sites appear to be camp-sites, often with remains of fish and animals strewn about the hearths. Qarunian tools were small-backed blades and bladelettes of the microlithic tradition. With the onset of lower Nile floods beginning about 5480 BC, the lake's water was no longer replenished. When the lake disappeared, the Qarunian culture disappeared as well: archaeologists have found no evidence of any occupation of the Fayyum basin for nearly 300 years, after which a fully Neolithic people occupied the shorelines of the revitalised lake. These people raised domestic animals and plants

---

BOX 4.2 ◆ Desert archaeology

When the author was working in the Fayyum and surrounding desert, the backed blades and finely flaked points so characteristic of the Qarunian and later Neolithic culture had absorbed so much of the sun's heat that by midday they could not be picked up or held comfortably with bare hands.

---

and resembled in many ways the early agricultural groups developing at this time in the Nile Delta.

The disappearance of Epi-paleolithic Qarunian culture and the sudden appearance of the Neolithic cultures are echoed all along the Nile Valley. How an agricultural lifestyle came to be adopted so quickly, however, is an open question. In even the earliest Neolithic sites, the agricultural lifestyle is fully developed, with the people living in villages, growing and harvesting wheat and barley and tending cattle, sheep, goats and pigs.

Without a doubt, an archaeological record of this revolutionary transition exists somewhere and is waiting to be found. Unfortunately, the evidence may lie under many metres of Nile silt. It is thought that the Nile was extremely low when the Fayyum's lake disappeared. People who were adapted to the Nile and living along its banks would have followed the river to its lower water level, camping near the shore to continue their activities. When the Nile returned to its higher levels, these campsites would have been inundated by water and covered by the silts deposited by the annual flood. So, although these important transitional sites probably exist, they are now located under metres of silt and water.

For the time being, the transition between Epi-paleolithic hunters and gatherers and the Neolithic agriculturalists remains a mystery. We know little about how or when domestic plants and animals spread into Egypt, but there are tantalising clues that agriculture was introduced into Egypt from the most unlikely of places – the deserts of the Sahara.

CHAPTER 5

• • • • • • • • • • • • • • •

The Neolithic:
An agricultural revolution
and new way of life

Some time around 7500–5000 BC, people in vastly different parts of the world (China, the Indus Valley, the Andes, Mesopotamia and Egypt) began shifting from a life based on hunting animals and gathering plants to one based on growing crops. Archaeologists call this period the Neolithic ('New Stone Age') and it has been accurately characterised as a revolution. It was this economic shift to food production, rather than simply hunting and collecting, that enabled people like the ancient Egyptians to amass great surpluses of food, which in turn permitted increases in population, craft specialisation and the construction of monumental public works. In fact, some scholars argue that agriculture has had a greater impact on human history than any other development.

Agriculture, which in its broadest sense includes domesticating animals as well as plants for human use, created the economic base that gave rise to the increasingly cooperative and centralised social interactions characteristic of all the early civilisations. Studies of modern populations involved in non-mechanised agriculture suggest, however, that relying on domestic crops is a precarious balancing act. Crop yields vary depending on rainfall and other uncontrollable natural conditions, and stored grain is susceptible to fire, water, pests and moulds. Moreover, life in crowded villages is often unsanitary, increasing the risk of infectious disease. To counter these potential hazards, some contemporary agricultural groups like those in Amazonia and New Guinea have adopted a mobile system of agriculture similar to the early Neolithic cultures of the Fayyum. For these groups, domestic crops serve as just one component of a broader food gathering strategy.

The negative effects of a life devoted to farming as opposed to hunting and gathering are further documented by ancient skeletal remains. Human skeletons from Greece and Turkey, for example, show that the average height of hunter-gatherers towards the end of the Ice Age (c.8000 BC) was about 172 cm (67.7 in.) for men and 162 cm (63.8 in.) for women. With the adoption of agriculture, average height plummeted to 157 cm (61.8 in.) and 150 cm (59 in.), respectively. By Classical times, heights were slowly rebounding, but not until modern times did Greeks and Turks regain the average height of their Paleolithic ancestors.

An even more graphic example of the effects of switching from a hunter-gatherer diet to a predominantly agricultural one comes from Native American remains in the Illinois and Ohio River valleys. Analyses of approximately 800 skeletons show that, compared with the hunter-gatherers who preceded them, the agriculturalists had a nearly 50 per cent increase in tooth enamel defects and a fourfold increase in iron deficiency anaemia, signalling malnutrition; a threefold rise in bone lesions, indicative of infectious disease in general; and an increase in degenerative conditions of the spine, probably reflecting a life of hard work.

In Egypt, the physical effects of the shift to agriculture are not well documented, but one study of Predynastic, Early Dynastic and Old Kingdom skeletons shows that Predynastic Egyptians suffered from anaemia and, with the exception of the elite, nearly all Early Dynastic and Old Kingdom Egyptians suffered from the same affliction. Such widespread anaemia has been attributed to poor hygienic conditions, particularly parasitic infestations, which are characteristic of crowded agricultural communities. Similarly, a study of the development of agriculture in Nubia showed nutritional deficiencies manifested by slow bone development, anaemia, micro-defects in dentition and premature osteoporosis in juveniles and young adult females.

With all these negative consequences, why would agriculture have been adopted in the first place? Possible catalysts include saturation of the ecosystems by hunter-gatherers or changes in the environment, human culture, or the biological make-up of the plants and animals. It is virtually impossible to delineate a single primary cause because many stimuli undoubtedly interacted to effect this transformation.

The most important clues to Egypt's shift to agriculture – the ancient plants and animals themselves – have proven to be controversial sources of information. Even working with the actual remains of early domestic species has provided only limited information and has actually fuelled the controversy rather than solved any mystery.

Plant and animal remains recovered through archaeological investigations are often identified by assessing their physical characteristics (size, shape and colour) and visually comparing the archaeological specimens with known wild and domestic examples. When working with seeds and bone fragments that have been subjected to thousands of years of aridity, erosion and in some cases fossilisation, comparisons can be difficult, and clear, unambiguous identifications are rare. Even when identifications of species can be made, determining whether or not the specimen is an early domesticate is almost impossible. Domestication is a long process based on genetic changes that may or may not affect the physical appearance of the plant or animal. Plants and animals at either end of the wild-to-domestic spectrum can be classified with some certainty, but those lying along the continuum are hard to identify. Consequently, claims for early domestication and agriculture rely on other, more unequivocal types of evidence such as:

- assessing the ecological fitness of a plant or animal vis-à-vis the local environment – that is, could the organism live in that area without the aid of humans?;
- studying the artefacts found in association with the remains, particularly with regard to their use as agricultural tools;
- identifying artistic renditions of plants and animals that are depicted on tools, ceramic vessels and other surfaces – in other words, is there graphic evidence of animals in domesticated contexts?

With respect to ancient Egypt, the wild progenitors of wheat, barley, sheep and goat (which, along with cattle and pig, formed the backbone of its domestic economy) were not indigenous. Most scholars therefore believe that many of the domestic species raised in Egypt originated

elsewhere and that Paleolithic Egyptians learned agriculture from neighbouring peoples.

Archaeological excavations at the site of Merimde in the Nile Delta
and at sites in the Fayyum have yielded undisputed evidence of domesticated plants and animals dating to approximately 5000 BC. Domesticated
sheep as well as the bones of cattle, pig and goat have been recovered
from the earliest levels of Merimde (5005 ± 125 BC). In the Fayyum, the
remains of domestic animals and a series of 168 grain silos containing
wheat (*Triticum dicorumm*) and two types of barley (*Hordeum hexas-
tichum* and *H. distichum*) have been dated to 5145 ± 155 years BC.

Rock art in Egypt's Western Desert also suggests an early use of
domestic plants and animals in the Sahara. Unfortunately, rock art is
seldom buried and thus cannot be dated using geological stratification.
It is also seldom found in association with other artefacts. (Even when
artefacts and drawings are seemingly found together, they can rarely be
linked with any degree of certainty.) Therefore, dating the desert rock art
depends on less precise methods such as:

- the internal composition of the picture (are extinct animals or
  datable artefacts shown?);
- the presence of dated inscriptions (useful for dating historical
  sites);
- the overlapping and cross-cutting relationships of different
  styles or themes (does one type of representation definitely and
  consistently overlie another?);
- general stylistic trends and patterns of artistic development
  (is there a consistent trend towards the stylisation of motifs?).

One of the most comprehensive works on Egypt's desert rock art was
compiled by the Swiss art historian Hans Winkler during the late 1930s.
Winkler collected and classified rock drawings from 40 different sites in
both the Western and Eastern Deserts, and he divided Egypt's desert
rock art into three categories: inscriptions, signs and pictures (Fig. 5.1a, b
and c). Although the inscriptions and signs were easy to date, the
pictures offered challenges. In an attempt to date the scenes and connect
them with particular peoples, he ascribed pictures to one of five periods:
Arab, Coptic, Greco-Roman, Dynastic, and undatable prehistoric or Early
Predynastic pictures of the Eastern and Western Deserts. Winkler made

FIGURE 5.1 ◆ *Winkler's rock art classification: (a) inscriptions; (b) signs.*

Source: Photographs by Patrick Richard Carstens

FIGURE 5.1 ♦ *(continued) Winkler's rock art classification: (c) pictures.*

Source: Photograph by D. J. Brewer

no attempt to separate engraved scenes from painted or inscribed but rather based his classification on the subjects depicted. His undatable desert categories were further broken down and attributed to four pre-historic groups: indigenous mountain dwellers, early Nile dwellers, eastern invaders and the earliest hunters. In an attempt to bring these prehistoric cultures to life, Winkler described each group of rock art in terms of its major characteristics, such as fauna, weapons, hunting practices, social life and religion. He even went so far as to propose ethnic divisions by comparing depictions of dress with that of modern peoples. By modern anthropological standards, he certainly pushed his interpretations beyond the evidence, but it must be acknowledged that he did distinguish some real differences in prehistoric desert art.

The most ancient rock drawings, as Winkler noted, are quite distinct from anything that came later. Animals, footprints of game, game traps and geometrical designs were standard motifs (Fig. 5.2). He believed the earliest hunters lived along the Nile, evidenced by drawings of crocodiles, and that they possessed dogs and used the bow and arrow (Fig. 5.3). Winkler thought these earliest hunters were succeeded by

FIGURE 5.2 ◆ *Earliest rock inscriptions are geometric designs and stylised animal footprints.*   *Source*: Courtesy of the Egypt Exploration Society

FIGURE 5.3 ◆ *Winkler's 'Nile hunters' carried bows and possessed domestic dogs.*   *Source*: Photograph by Patrick Richard Carstens

FIGURE 5.4 ◆ *Scenes of indigenous mountain dwellers and their cattle, many of which focus on the udder: Winkler's clue that milk was an important product of cattle herding.* Source: Courtesy of the Egypt Exploration Society

cattle pastoralists, which he named 'indigenous mountain dwellers' because he believed they were speakers of an ancient Hamitic language (a group that includes ancient Egyptian and modern Berber) who emigrated from the Nile Valley out on to the Eastern and Western Deserts. Although the rock drawings suggested to Winkler that these cattle pastoralists still hunted wild animals like ibex, antelope and ostrich, he thought that the most commonly depicted animals – long-horned cattle – were thoroughly domesticated (Plate 7). He based this conclusion on drawings showing the artificial deformation of the cattle's horns (a practice known in ancient Egypt) and on the care the artists took in representing the udder, which suggested that they were using these cattle for milk (Fig. 5.4).

A comparison of the frequency of animals depicted in paintings with those in engravings led a later scholar, William McHugh, to conclude that engraved hunting scenes preceded painted pastoral scenes. In his analysis, he stressed that the paintings and engravings Winkler tabulated portrayed significantly different species. Although cattle are the most

EGYPT

Nile

Nabta
Playa

FIGURE 5.5 ◆ *Map showing
the Nabta Playa. (See Fig. 4.5
for a view of the playa.)*
Source: Redrawn by Brenda Coelho

abundant individual species in both types of rock art, they comprise almost 98 per cent of the animals depicted in Winkler's painted scenes compared with only 32 per cent in the engravings. On the other hand, wild animals (excluding jackals, as it is difficult to separate them from domestic dogs) comprise 62 per cent of all animals in the engraved scenes but only 2 per cent of those in the painted scenes.

Although rock art does provide tantalising clues about some of Egypt's earliest pastoralists, the evidence is not indisputable. New and even more compelling evidence for the earliest use of domestic plants and animals in Egypt comes from recent archaeological excavations in Egypt's Nabta Playa, located deep in the Western Desert (Figs 5.5 and 4.5). Here, bones believed to be those of domestic cattle were recovered in direct association with cultural materials thought to be nearly 10,000 years old. The argument for these remains' being domesticated animals is built, however, on ecological criteria rather than on the morphology of the recovered skeletal elements because the recovered cattle bones are indistinguishable from those of wild cattle. Researchers have postulated that the environment, which supported hare and gazelle whose bones were also recovered, was too arid to support cattle, which have greater water requirements for survival. Therefore, cattle could only exist in the area if tended by humans.

What Nabta suggests and what the rock art tends to support is that domestic animals and plants might have been present in the desert as early as or even earlier than in the Nile Valley.

Within the context of Nabta living sites, ash from fire hearths produced a rich assortment of plant remains. Clearly, the hearths were being used as cooking pits. Plants identified include legumes, grass grains, mustard seeds, nabk berries (Christ thorn), millet and sorghum. Seed size and structure, however, all correspond to known wild races. Interestingly, today these species occur naturally in the arid savanna some 600–700 km (372.8–434.9 miles) south of Nabta, suggesting that a northerly shift of the savanna had occurred by 6000 BC. Furthermore, although the plant remains recovered appeared to be morphologically identical to wild forms, spectrographic analysis of sorghum grains and a study of their lipids suggest the possibility that at least the sorghum might have been cultivated.

Studies suggest that an opportunistic and mobile desert lifestyle, like that practised by the Epi-paleolithic and early Neolithic inhabitants of the Fayyum, may have been a key factor in the adoption of domestic plants and animals. In general, both Fayyum groups maintained a mobile hunting and gathering way of life, but during the Neolithic domesticated animals and plants were added to an already broad and diversified hunting and gathering lifestyle. The new agricultural resources served as additional insurance against an increasingly unpredictable food supply brought on by the more arid conditions that prevailed after 6000 BC. A complete reliance on domestic plants and animals was not practical because of the increasingly arid climate and unpredictable yields, but, by simply adding new agricultural products to the wild species already used, Neolithic Egyptians attained an even broader overall survival strategy. Put simply, domesticated plants and animals added new alternative food resources to an already diverse group of wild foods, thereby adding an additional line of insurance against famine.

A mixed strategy such as this would also have worked well in the Western Desert in areas such as the Nabta Playa. Groups here were not sedentary but practised seasonal migration to take advantage of different food resources as they became available. Initially, cattle, and later sheep and goat, were probably herded by the migrating people. By planting a few crops in well-watered areas along the way, they added an additional food resource. Also, as in modern nomadic groups, the entire population did not necessarily move each season. Cultivated plants might have been abandoned until harvest, or they may have been tended for part or all of the growing season. Some groups may have even been semi-permanently settled, like those in the late Neolithic Fayyum, where it is thought some members lived at one site year-round.

Initially, people living along the Nile had little use for domesticated plants and animals because the area was rich in wild resources. Fish and fowl were plentiful and predictable, and large animals could be taken on the grasslands near the river. However, as the areas west and east of the Nile became increasingly more arid, groups living in these regions migrated to the Nile and to Egypt's major oases, such as Kharga and Dakhla, which served as refuges, and this new wave of people brought domestic plants and animals. As populations grew and congregated, the most easily cultivated areas became scarce and the diversified hunting–gathering lifestyle eventually gave way to more intensive food production. Agriculture, because it offered greater productivity for a given tract of land, became a more viable option for maintaining a stable source of food for a growing population. Shifting to an agricultural economy was not, however, without pitfalls. Depending on fewer food species increased the risk of famine, should crops fail. But in a typical year, crop yields were large enough not only to feed the growing population but to offer a storable surplus as well. With agriculture now established, villages appeared and grew in size, and local leaders emerged in response to the need for administrative decisions such as how much surplus food should be stored for times of need or for how to arrange labour for community projects like irrigation improvements. In short, a new era in Egyptian prehistory had begun: the Predynastic.

CHAPTER 6

• • • • • • • • • • • • • •

The Predynastic Period: Egypt in its infancy

The Predynastic (*c.*4400 BC) spans the time from the introduction of farming to the unification of the country under the first king of Dynasty 1 (3050 BC). In a sense, it is defined by a set of artificial boundaries created by scholars to distinguish an ill-defined line between the earlier Neolithic and the more complexly organised later Dynastic culture. The boundaries defining this period are artificial in that the developing cultures progressed along a continuum – they were not separated by a single notable event – and some sites classified by archaeologists as Predynastic had strong Neolithic or Early Dynastic aspects. For example, the Early Predynastic Badarian culture still employed Neolithic subsistence methods and Neolithic Merimde had numerous Predynastic characteristics (albeit different from Upper Egypt because of the Delta's environmental influences). Regardless, the term Predynastic signifies that period when Egyptians developed the cultural vitality and complexity that enabled them to deal as equals with the dazzling civilisations of the Levant and Near East – and later to surpass those cultures. The most impressive yet puzzling aspect of this period is the cultural transformation itself: how did agricultural villages coalesce into regional political units and then unite to create the first great nation-state in history?

As with the transition from hunting and gathering to agricultural village life, we know little about this process. Equally as intriguing is the possibility that foreign contacts and long-distance trade played some role in Egypt's development at this time. One of the difficulties in understanding this period and its transformations is the nature of the data used for interpretation. Although ancient Egyptian texts such as the Turin King List and Palermo Stone make vague reference to events that predate Dynasty I, material remains such as pottery, stoneware, jewellery, animal bones and plant remains provide the majority of our evidence. These artefacts are excellent for establishing long-term trends but much less accurate when used to define singular significant events in prehistory.

It is clear that by Predynastic times Nile geography influenced social development differently in the north from in the south, such that distinctive cultural identities had evolved in the Delta and Valley proper (see Table 2.1). Geography also influenced archaeological preservation and thus modern-day research. The Upper Egyptian Nile Valley, with its well-drained flood plain and adjacent dry desert, offered excellent preservation and the area has produced the vast majority of archaeological information we have to interpret these early cultures. The Delta, on the other hand, because of its humid environment and high water table (and consequent poor preservation of artefacts), has only recently been the target of extensive research and excavations. This has resulted in a poor balance of knowledge: we know much more about the evolution of Upper Egypt than about that of Lower Egypt.

The Predynastic was first introduced to the archaeological community in 1896, when Jacques de Morgan (Fig. 2.3), excavating the cemeteries of Abydos, recovered bone and ivory jewellery and figurines, slate palettes, beautiful flaked flint tools and pottery of a style different from that of the later Dynastic Period (Plates 8 and 9). De Morgan asserted that these graves and those from other nearby sites predated Dynasty 1 – a particularly profound declaration for him to make without any stratigraphic or other corroborating evidence. Luckily, he was correct.

Despite his precociousness, de Morgan did not follow up his assertion with further work. Rather, it took the now famous British archaeologist William Flinders Petrie's organisational skills and years of study to prove de Morgan correct. The greatest problem facing Petrie was the immense size of the Predynastic cemeteries at Naqada, Ballas, Abadiyeh and Hu. At Naqada, for example, a total of 2,149 graves were packed into a single cemetery. In taking advantage of the soft subsoil on desert spurs overlooking the Nile Valley (Fig. 6.1), the prehistoric Naqadans laid their dead side by side and spaced so closely together that the area was saturated

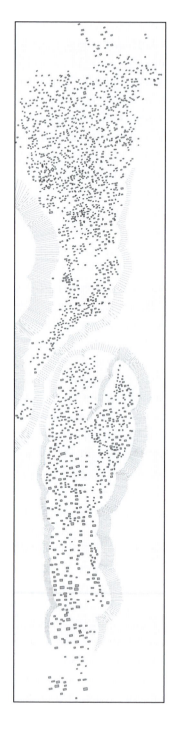

FIGURE 6.1 ◆ *Each tiny square represents a grave in Petrie's Naqada cemetery. Located on a desert spur, the area was virtually saturated with thousands of Predynastic graves.*

Source: After Brewer, Redford and Redford, *Domesticated Plants and Animals: The Egyptian Origins* (Aris and Phillips, 1991). Courtesy of Oxbow Books. Redrawn by Brenda Coelho

with bodies. The Naqada cemetery, located on the west bank of the Nile, foreshadowed the Pharaonic Egyptians' concept of the land of the dead located towards the setting sun.

After six years of hard work studying the many artefacts recovered from Naqada and other nearby sites, Petrie made archaeological history in 1901 by assigning relative dates to the thousands of graves he and his assistants had unearthed. Without written records and without the benefit of modern techniques such as carbon-14 dating, he had reconstructed a complex sequence of Predynastic grave goods reflecting the passage of time.

His ingenious technique of sequence dating was based on two steps: first he split broad categories of artefacts such as pottery into several types. Next he noted which types of artefacts were always found together. By assigning a sequential number from 30 to 80 for each object, based upon its stylistic complexity, he ordered them in a sequence from youngest to oldest (Fig. 6.2). (By ranging his finds from 30 to 80 he left space for future discoveries.) The success of Petrie's system was based on how well he could determine the correct direction a given artistic or technological characteristic evolved. For example, he made much out of the fact that wavy-handles on certain ceramic vessels declined in size through a series of stages (also see Plate 1) until they became useless decorative motifs moulded in low relief or simply painted on the side of jars. How did he know the functional handles were earliest and the decorative ones latest? As Petrie himself said, he just used his own intuition.

Two years later, de Morgan, excavating at Naqada, unearthed the tomb of Queen Neith-hotep and found ceramic vessels with non-functional decorative handles (No. 80 in Petrie's sequence – the end of the Predynastic sequence) in association with ivory labels that bore the name of Aha, a king of Dynasty 1 – proof that Petrie was correct and that his sequence dating system worked. By employing his system, archaeologists could now take a given object, compare it with Petrie's list and immediately assign it a relative date.

As other sites were discovered in Upper and Lower Egypt, a detailed Predynastic sequence began to be developed, as well as an understanding that Upper and Lower Egypt underwent different cultural developments. Scholars have divided the cultural sequence for Upper and Lower Egypt into four periods. The sequence for Upper Egypt begins with Badarian

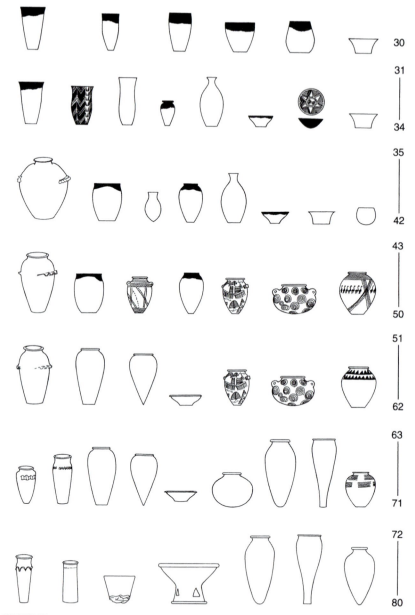

FIGURE 6.2 ◆ *Petrie's ceramic sequence and its associated 'sequence date'.*
He purposely left space at the beginning and end of his chronology (0–30 and
80–100) for future discoveries.

Source: After Brewer, Douglas J. and Teeter,
Emily, *Egypt and the Egyptians* (Cambridge University Press, 1999)

and continues through Naqada I, Naqada II and Naqada III. The sequence for Lower Egypt begins with the Fayyum/Merimde Neolithic, followed by Omari and Ma'adian, ending as in Upper Egypt with the Naqada III Period (Table 2.1).

Upper Egypt

The Badarian

The Badarian culture (c.4400–4000 BC), the earliest element of the Upper Egyptian Predynastic sequence, marks a lifestyle radically different from what preceded it. We suddenly find ourselves in a symbolic universe of incredible richness, reflecting an increasingly structured and complex society, a process that accelerates through the next 1,000 years, eventually culminating in the First Dynasty of a united Egypt.

Although the Badarian civilisation was limited to a 35 km (21.7 miles) stretch of the Nile centred near the site of el-Badari, Badarian artefacts have been found as far south as Hierakonpolis and as far north as Armont. A Badarian cemetery was even found in the Wadi Hammamat, suggesting regular contact with the Eastern Desert and Red Sea.

Like later Predynastic cultures, the Badarian exhibited a tendency towards ornamentation and display that distinguished it from contemporaneous groups in the Western Desert and Delta. Badarian pottery was well made and frequently decorated. Rectangular and oval slate palettes often bear traces of red ochre or green malachite, revealing their use as grinding surfaces, while pots have been found filled with prepared pigment. Beautifully made hollow-based projectile points, found here and in the Fayyum and Lower Egypt, suggest contact between these areas. Badarian graves held countless shell and stone bead necklaces, as well as well-made ivory spoons, humanoid figurines of clay or ivory, animal amulets and carved throwing sticks used to propel darts in hunting (see Fig. 6.4). A few graves contained small copper tools and ornamental pins. These were hammered or annealed rather than cast, as they were in other areas of the Middle East, where copper metallurgy was already 1,000 years old.

Most Badarian graves took the form of simple oval pits, each with a single individual. With few exceptions, bodies were in a contracted or

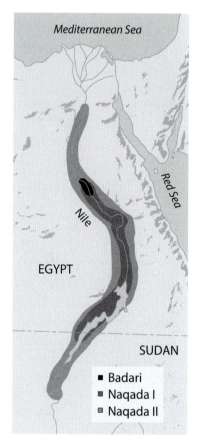

FIGURE 6.3 ◆ *The approximate extent of the Badari, Naqada I and II cultural regions.*

Source: Redrawn by Brenda Coelho

fetal position, on their left side with the head oriented to the south and facing west (Fig. 6.5). Occasionally, graves contained more than one body; often such graves held an adult and a newborn infant.

Each burial was carefully arranged. A mat was placed at the bottom of the pit to keep the body off the bare earth, and the head was sometimes laid on a straw or rolled-up animal skin pillow. The body was then covered or wrapped with a mat or animal skin (possibly gazelle). In a few cases, a piece of cloth was placed between the animal skin and the body. Most of the time it appears that this skin also covered one or more pottery vessels placed as a funerary offering, but in some graves pots were placed at a higher level, as if they had not been added to the burial until the body itself had been at least partly interred. Remains of clothes suggest that the deceased were buried in a short loincloth made from linen or animal skin

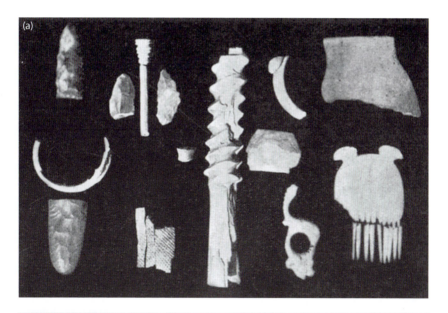

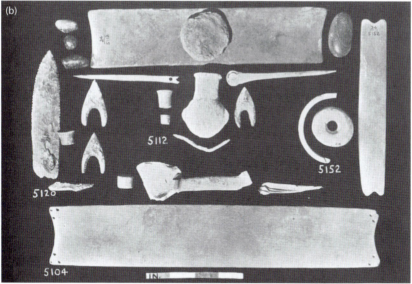

FIGURE 6.4 ◆ *Typical Badarian artefacts for procuring and producing food, adorning their bodies and expressing their creativity and craftsmanship.*

Source: Courtesy of the Egypt Exploration Society

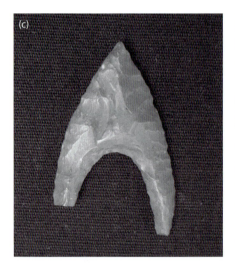

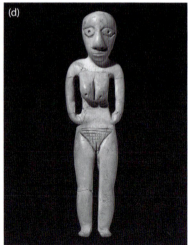

FIGURE 6.4 ◆ *(continued) Typical Badarian artefacts: (c) hollow base point; (d) ivory figurine*

Sources: (c) Photograph by D. J. Brewer;
(d) © Copyright The British Museum

FIGURE 6.5 ◆ *Oval pit graves from the defining Badarian excavations of the early 20th century.* *Source*: Courtesy of the Egypt Exploration Society

lined with linen. Siltstone grinding palettes were often placed in direct association with the body, sometimes bearing traces of ochre or malachite stains, and many were accompanied by stone grinders of various types.

Although no wooden coffins have been found, reeds have been excavated from the soil surrounding the burials, suggesting that some bodies may have been wrapped in a kind of armature that would also have served as a form of roofing for the graves. In one case, a small wickerwork receptacle seems to have held the remains of a young child, with pottery vessels found outside the rudimentary coffin. Thus far, only one burial here included a small separate room for funerary offerings.

The pottery vessels placed by the side of the deceased constitute the most distinguishing element of the Badarian culture. Pots were fashioned by hand and the outside surface of the vessel was combed with a serrated implement (before firing), producing a rippled effect on the finished pot (Plate 10).

Other characteristic Badarian grave goods were ivory and bone combs with long teeth surmounted by a stylised animal motif (Fig. 6.4a). The frequent occurrence of pins and awls made from bird bones and of curved and straight-eye needles implies the working of hides and textiles. Ivory formed the basis for an important craft industry that included bracelets, bead rings, small rods sculpted in spirals (whose purpose is uncertain), spoons and cylindrical vessels for cosmetics. Wooden items consisted of small, pointed, straight and curved sticks, possibly used for working hides. Ostrich eggs were used as vessels and as raw material for beads (Fig. 6.6). Pierced Red Sea shells, copper, steatite and stones carved into disc shapes were popular ornaments for necklaces.

Compared with the wealth of their graves, Badarian settlement remains seem somewhat impoverished. Sites lack architectural remains, supporting the notion that this was a semi-sedentary society, probably pastoral, living on the Nile alluvium but far enough away from the river so that their villages were not inundated by the annual flood. One important structural feature that has been preserved at Badarian sites is silos, often large jars buried in the soil (Fig. 6.7). Evidently, like the Fayyum cultures, Badarians took advantage of the lands nearer permanent water for growing crops to store, primarily wheat and barely.

We have only a vague idea of the animals the Badarian people used, but the remains of cattle, sheep, antelope, cats and dogs have been

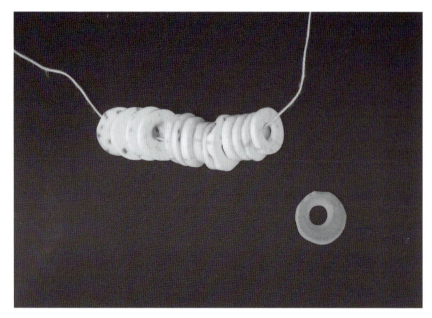

FIGURE 6.6 ◆ *An ostrich eggshell bead in profile and as a strung series for a necklace.* *Sources*: Courtesy of the Spurlock Museum, University of Illinois

FIGURE 6.7 ◆ *A large sunken ceramic vessel employed as a Badarian grain silo.* *Source*: Courtesy of the Egypt Exploration Society

recovered. It is highly probable that these represent domesticated forms. In fact, wrapped burials of antelope, dogs and sheep were found at the site of Badari, and animal skulls were commonly found next to the bodies of the interred. Plant remains included barley, wheat and the castor bean plant. A study of the lithic material shows that Badarians used a wide range of tools, such as scrapers, burins, perforators and finely made arrowheads and sickles.

Badarians were the first people in Egypt to use copper. Hammered copper was used for pins and beads, the latter either cylindrical, made by rolling a pounded piece of copper, or ring-like, made from a single strand twisted into a spiral. It is likely that metallic objects were more widespread than our archaeological evidence suggests. Traces of green oxidation can be seen on the remains of leather bags, suggesting copper ornaments were once affixed, but probably later stolen by tomb robbers or simply disintegrated over time.

There were three potential sources of copper: the Sinai, the Eastern Desert and the Sudan. The closest source, the Eastern Desert, does not appear to have been utilised until the Pharaonic Period, and little evidence exists for copper entering Egypt from the Sudan in the south. The most likely source for Badarian copper appears to be the Sinai, where cultures native to Palestine were known to work copper as well as turquoise. Interestingly, no contemporary traces of copper have been found in the Delta, suggesting a more direct trade route between the Palestinian copper-producing cultures and the Badarians. Such a route probably went through the Wadi Hammamat, which connects the Badari region to the Red Sea coast, where Badarian artefacts and a Badarian cemetery have been recovered.

Where did the Badarians come from? Because Badarians shared cultural elements with peoples of the Desert, Delta, Nubia and Southwest Asia, scholars have looked to each of these areas as a possible source. Given all the evidence, however, the simplest explanation is that Badarians did not come from somewhere else but were an indigenous Egyptian people whose complex culture evolved from their surrounding environment. This can be seen in their lithic technology, which was perfectly adapted to the local sources of flint. All other elements of their culture were similarly *in situ* adaptations, although the concepts themselves might have been introduced from other areas. As contacts with neighbouring regions intensified through trade for exotic goods such as turquoise, copper, steatite and seashells, ideas were surely also exchanged.

Naqada I

The Naqada I culture (originally referred to as Amratian: see Table 2.1) is represented by numerous sites, from Matmar in the north to Wadi Kubbaniya and Khor Bahan in the south. Based on the density of materials, the heartland of the Naqada I culture was near the site of el-Amra in the Naqada Mahasna region. From this core, the Naqada I culture expanded northward into territory traditionally associated with the Badarian and southward 20 km (12.4 miles) beyond the first Nile cataract.

When considering Naqada I origins, there is no sharp or distinct cultural break between the Badarians and Naqadans. Like the Neolithic-Predynastic transition, some early Naqada I sites contain Badarian elements and some late Badarian sites contain some Naqada I elements. This would suggest an indigenous development for the Naqada culture, but it is not known whether Badarian evolved into Naqada I or whether both cultures had independent sources that later merged. Badarian is the earlier culture, but the occurrence of shared traits in otherwise classic Naqada I or Badarian sites suggests some coexistence, with the Naqada I culture eventually prevailing.

In essence, many aspects of the Naqada I culture were similar to the Badarian. The dead were buried on their left side, in a contracted position, with the head to the south and facing westward. But at this time we begin to see a small proportion of bodies being buried in large well-equipped graves rather than simple pits. Wrapping the body in animal skins was less common and wooden and clay coffins made their first appearance, although still rare. As in the Badarian, men, women and children were buried throughout the cemetery without any sense of zoning. Black-topped red ware pottery, a Predynastic hallmark, made its debut at this time (Plates 11 and 12). The Badarian combed or rippling pottery treatment still existed but soon faded out of style, while red polished pottery became increasingly more common (Plate 13). The diversity of vessel shapes similarly increased at this time, probably reflecting a wider use of ceramic vessels for different purposes.

FIGURE 6.8 ◆ *An abbreviated list of pot marks recorded on early Naqada vessels. Note how some marks resemble early hieroglyphs.*

Source: After Petrie, W. M. F., *Naqada and Ballas* (Aris and Phillips, 1974).
Courtesy Oxbow Books. Redrawn by Brenda Coelho

A new feature of the pottery dated to this period is that many vessels were incised with signs known as pot-marks, usually made after firing (Fig. 6.8 and Plate 14). The fact that the same signs were repeated on different pots within particular graves suggests that they might have been a manufacturer's mark or symbols of vessel ownership. A large number of

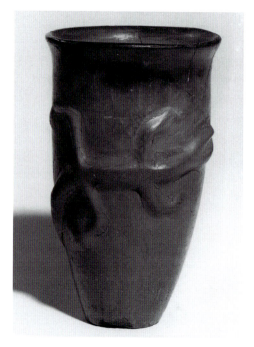

FIGURE 6.9 ◆ *An interesting artefact of the Naqada I Period is the animal relief pot. Figures are moulded on the side of the vessel.*

Source: © Copyright The British Museum

different mark designs exists, ranging from figurative (humans, animals, boats) to abstract (triangles, crescents, arrows).

The red polished vessels were occasionally decorated with white painted designs (Plates 15 and 16), comprising geometrical, animal and vegetal motifs. The fauna represented on the vessels included crocodiles, hippos and desert animals such as scorpions, gazelle, giraffes and bovids. The human form was also depicted, although with less frequency than animals (Plate 17). In a very significant development, animals were made to stand out from the surface of the vessel in a kind of raised relief decoration (Fig. 6.9).

The human form was also represented in three dimensions as a figurine (Fig. 6.10). Figurines were usually made of clay, but some made of ivory and bone exist. The figurines appear to be grave offerings, but their meaning remains unclear. The reason so little is known of their symbolic significance is that only about one-third of the known examples have been recovered through scholarly excavations, the vast majority being recovered from art dealers or from looters. What we do know is

FIGURE 6.10 ◆ *The human form is rarely depicted in the Naqada I Period but is sometimes moulded from clay.*

Source: © Petrie Museum of Egyptian
Archaeology, University College London

that they were rare, usually found singly (although one tomb contained 16 figurines), and that the tombs in which they have been found were not overly rich in grave goods, the figurine often being the sole offering.

Another characteristic Naqada I artefact is the disc-shaped mace head (Fig. 6.11). They were usually carved from hard stone, but examples in soft limestone, pottery and even unfired clay also survive. The fact that many of these were non-functional replicas suggests that they were portable symbols of power rather than true weapons.

Stone carving extended to vessels, which at this time were primarily made from soft stone, their shapes being more or less cylindrical, with a conical base and two handles pierced vertically to facilitate their transport (Fig. 6.12). Stone grinding palettes also began to appear in a great diversity of shapes (Fig. 6.13). Artists also incorporated animal features into the palette's overall shape, using incisions to emphasise certain details. This bestiary included fish, turtles and crocodiles, as well as birds, hippos and elephants. The fact that the palettes were sometimes perforated suggests that they were carried or worn by an individual during life or may have been tied to the corpse in preparation for burial.

FIGURE 6.11 ◆ *A disc-shaped mace head characteristic of the early Naqada Period. This fine example is made of dark grey and white porphyry.*

Source: © Petrie Museum of Egyptian Archaeology, University College London

Bone and ivory carving also flourished at this time, and archaeologists have recovered punches, needles, awls, long-toothed combs with decorated handles, hairpins, bracelets, rings and small vessels shaped like those made from stone.

Stone tools are rare in Naqada I graves, but those that have been recovered tend to have been worked to a very high standard. These include delicate bifacially worked blades, some nearly 40 cm (15.7 in.) in length (Fig. 6.14). Naqada I stone tools were not restricted to these fine decorative or ceremonial examples; many utilitarian tools were also made. Although arrow heads were rare, bifacial sickles, many with a silica sheen (Fig. 6.15) indicating they were used for cutting grasses such as wheat and barley, were common, suggesting an increased role of cereal grains in the food supply and a decreasing role for hunting.

In this period, Egyptians first attempted to create faïence, a quartz-based blue or blue-green matrix often used to make small statues and

FIGURE 6.12 ◆ *Examples of the excellence achieved by Naqada I stone-workers. These vessels, like much of the stone working of the day, were made from soft stones such as limestone and breccia.*

Source: © Petrie Museum of Egyptian Archaeology, University College London

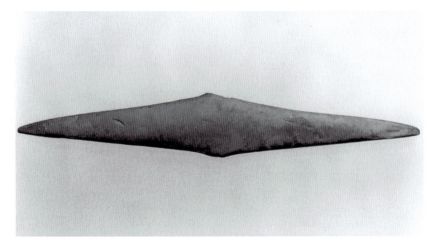

FIGURE 6.13 ◆ *A double-pointed slate palette measuring 56.6 cm (22 in.) long. Geometric shaped palettes and palettes formed into animal shapes were common in the Naqada I Period. Such palettes are thought to have been used for grinding cosmetics and other related preparations.*

Source: © Brooklyn Museum of Art

FIGURE 6.14 ◆ *A beautiful ripple-flaked blade measuring nearly 40 cm (15.7 in.) long. After the Naqada Period this delicate craft seems to have disappeared and the skills required to create it seem to have been lost.*

Source: © Petrie Museum of Egyptian Archaeology, University College London

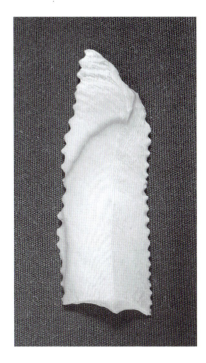

FIGURE 6.15 ◆ *Sickle blade with the characteristic denticulated cutting edge.*
Source: Courtesy of the Spurlock Museum, University of Illinois

amulets. The technical process involved shaping a nucleus of crushed quartz into the desired form and then applying a coat of natron-based glaze, coloured by a blue-green metallic oxide (Plate 18). Interestingly, control over the high temperatures needed to make faïence suggests that the skills for metalworking existed, but the Naqada I people, like the earlier Badarians, did not forge copper; they merely hammered it into shapes. Copper objects included pins, harpoons, beads, bracelets, anklets and even a few fishhooks and spear tips.

Our first glimpse of an Egyptian dwelling and village comes from the Naqada I Period, at Hememia, where we find circular mud and reed huts varying from about 1 to 1.25 metre (3.28–4.1 ft) in diameter (Fig. 6.16). Although the smaller structures were probably storage facilities, the larger ones included traces of fire hearths, suggesting these were living quarters. Recent work on the Naqada I sites of the Khattara area suggests that the area's villages ranged in size from several hundred square metres to several hectares. At any one time throughout its 200-year occupation, the village population probably did not exceed 50–200 people.

FIGURE 6.16 ◆ *Artistic rendition of a Naqada village with circular homes and*
outbuildings.   *Source*: After Aldred, C. A. *Egypt to the End of the Old Kingdom,*
(Thames and Hudson, 1965)

The Naqada I diet included sheep, goat, pig and cattle, as well as wild
game such as gazelle and fish. Barley and wheat were cultivated, along
with legumes, and a fodder plant was grown to supplement the herd
animal's diet.

At Hierakonpolis we get our first glimpse of the intricate dynamics of
Naqada I life. Here archaeologists have uncovered the remains of a type
of kiln or oven and a charred rectangular house (as opposed to circular)
(Fig. 6.17). The kiln measured about 5 by 6 metres (16.4 by 19.7 ft) and
contained a significant quantity of the remains of large jars with diame-
ters ranging from 50 to 100 cm (19.69 to 39.37 in.). There was also evidence that a fire from the kiln spread to the neighbouring rectangular
home, which measured 4 by 3.5 metres (11.48 ft), with a foundation and
first floor about 40–80 cm (15.75–31.50 in.) below the surface. Its walls,
supported by wooden posts, had been plastered with a mixture of mud,

FIGURE 6.17 ◆ *Hierakonpolis kiln (a) and a house (b) that were destroyed by an out-of-control kiln fire. Archaeologists have speculated on the cause of the blaze, the most likely scenario being a wayward flame or spark from the kiln. Notice the burnt roof support beam (centre left of house image) lying where it fell more than 5,000 years ago.*   Source: © Jeremy Geller

dung and mud brick rubble. Based on wall and post height, the roof probably stood about 1.45 metres high. A series of smaller posts outside the house suggested that a light fence had enclosed the surrounding area. Inside the house were an oven, a mud platform, a storage pot and a large upside down vessel, all of which indicate cooking activities.

Clearly, based on the Hierakonpolis evidence, rectangular homes, some perhaps made of mud brick, were in use by Naqada I times. But how do they relate to the circular huts found at other Naqada I sites? This variety in dwelling styles probably reflects the increasing economic and social diversity of the times. The lighter circular huts, for example, might have served the poorer sector of the populace, or they might have been temporary dwellings for pastoralists or others who needed to relocate frequently; the sturdier mud brick homes might have served the wealthy or those with more permanently based occupations, such as potters and other craftsmen.

Naqada II

El-Gerza, the type-site for the Naqada II culture, lies 5 km (3.1 miles) north of the Meidum Pyramid, which attests to this second phase of the Naqada culture as one of geographical expansion. Naqada II (or Gerzean) sites extend from el-Gerza, near the Fayyum, south into Nubia. The wide range of funerary practices in Naqada II cemeteries – small round, oval or rectangular pits with varying amounts of grave goods, burials inside pottery vessels, different types of body wrappings and coffins – all reflect the growing complexity of Egyptian society, which was becoming both more diversified and more hierarchical. Based primarily on cemetery finds, the Naqada II culture appears to be one of increasing social diversity coupled with a consolidation of wealth and power into fewer hands.

The average Gerzean burial was a simple pit-grave containing a single corpse (Fig. 6.18). Sometimes an inhumation might include two bodies, but rarely more. The corpse was usually found in a fetal position, but the precise position of the body varied from one cemetery to the next. Wrapping the body in an animal skin was rare; instead, mats or linen cloth were more often used. Children began to be buried in large pottery vessels (sometimes upturned) and wealthier adults were interred in coffins, which were initially made from basketry, then clay and finally

PLATE 1 ◆ *Petrie's wavy-handled jar sequence, from the early form with a functional handle to later forms with only a decorative motif.*

Source: © Carnegie Museum of Natural History

PLATE 2 ◆ *Satellite image of the east central delta showing Predynastic sites. The black rectangular areas near the centre of the image represent ancient mud brick walls.*

Source: Brewer Research

PLATE 3 ◆ *Agricultural fields along the fertile Nile Valley.*

Source: Photograph by Patrick Richard Carstens

PLATE 4 ◆ *The Upper Nile Valley near the town of Beni Suef in Middle Egypt.*

Source: Photograph by D. J. Brewer

PLATE 5 ◆ *Nile cataracts near Aswan.*

Source: Photograph by Patrick Richard Carstens

PLATE 6 ◆ *The clear contrast between Egypt's rich agricultural land and the desert.*

Source: Photograph by D. J. Brewer

PLATE 7 ◆ *Indigenous mountain dwellers and their cattle.*

PLATE 8 ◆ *Examples of classic Naqada Period artefacts.*

PLATE 9 ◆ *Examples of classic Naqada Period pottery.*

PLATE 10 ◆ *The hallmark 'rippled pottery' of the Badarian culture. The ripple effect is made by dragging a serrated catfish spine or comb across the unfired clay vessel, then smoothing the marks with well-watered hands and firing the pot.*

PLATE 11 AND PLATE 12 ◆ *The classic Naqada I ceramic type is black-topped red ware. The distinctive black top is created by upturning the vessel and placing the top in the kiln fuel. After the vessel is fully fired the lack of oxygen within the burning fuel results in the shiny black colouring.*

Source: © Petrie Museum of Egyptian Archaeology, University College London

PLATE 13 ◆ *Naqada I red ware is similar to its black-topped counterpart but it has not been fired in kiln fuel in the upturned position.*

Source: © Petrie Museum of Egyptian Archaeology, University College London

PLATE 14 ◆ *Example of a Naqada I pot mark.*

Source: © Petrie Museum of Egyptian Archaeology, University College London

PLATE 15 AND PLATE 16 ◆ *Naqada I white cross-lined pottery with geometric designs.*

Source: © Petrie Museum of Egyptian Archaeology, University College London

PLATE 17 ◆ *Naqada I pottery with dancing (?) human figures.*
Source: © Petrie Museum of Egyptian Archaeology, University College London

PLATE 18 ◆ *One of the earliest examples of Egyptian faïence.*
Source: © Carnegie Museum of Natural History

PLATE 19 ◆ *Naqada II pottery: pink ware with geometric designs.*
Source: Squat jar with lug handles. Egypt, Predynastic Period, Naqada IIb Period.
*c.*4000–3000 BC. Marl clay, D. 23.50 cm. © The Cleveland Museum of Art,
Gift of the John Huntington Art and Polytechnic Trust, 1920.19879.

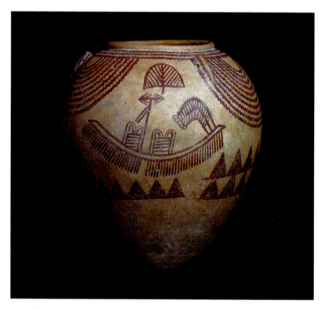

PLATE 20 ◆ *Naqada II pottery: pink ware with scenic designs.*
Source: Decorated jar with boat scene. Egypt, Late Predynastic Period,
Naqada IIc–d Periods, 4000–3000 BC. Pottery, marl clay, D. 28.20 cm. © The Cleveland
Museum of Art, Gift of the John Huntington Art and Polytechnic Trust, 1914.639.

PLATE 21 ◆ *Pink ware with scenic designs.*   *Source*: © Brooklyn Museum of Art

PLATE 22 ◆ *Naqada II stone vessel.*

Source: © Petrie Museum of Egyptian Archaeology, University College London

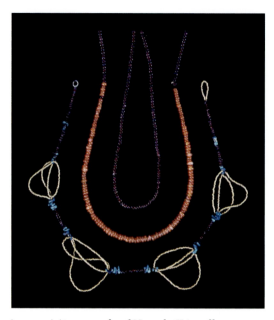

PLATE 23 ◆ *An exquisite example of Naqada II jewellery.*

PLATE 24 ◆ *Clay female figurine positioned in a pose very similar to those found on Naqada II pottery.*

PLATE 25 ◆ *The simple kilt was worn throughout the Dynastic Period by men of all classes. Decorative borders and finer linen were employed for the upper classes.* *Source*: Photograph by D. J. Brewer

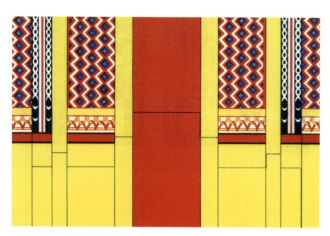

PLATE 26 ◆ *Decorated façade niching found on an Early Dynastic Saqqara* mastaba. *It is not known if such decorations were also applied to Upper Egyptian* mastabas. *Source*: Courtesy of the Egypt Exploration Society

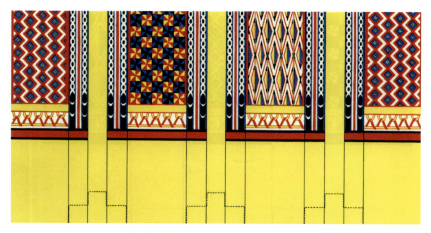

PLATE 27 ◆ *Decorated façade niching found on an Early Dynastic Saqqara* mastaba. *It is not known if such decorations were also applied to Upper Egyptian* mastabas. *Source*: Courtesy of the Egypt Exploration Society

PLATE 28 ◆ *This faïence tile wall was a feature of the Saqqara Step Pyramid* *and is thought to represent Early Dynastic coloured reed mats that would have* *been in mud-brick homes and tombs.* *Source*: Photograph by D. J. Brewer

PLATE 29 ◆ *The Upper Nile Valley near Luxor (ancient Thebes).*

Source: Photograph by Patrick Richard Carstens

PLATE 30 ◆ *The wall mural from the famous Lost Tomb (Tomb 100) of Hierakonpolis.*

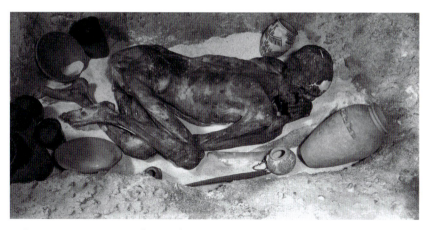

FIGURE 6.18 ◆ *A typical Naqada II pit grave with the deceased placed in a crouched position, head to the south and looking to the west. Characteristic period ceramic vessels accompany the deceased in her final resting place.*

Source: © Copyright The British Museum

wood (Fig. 6.19). The switch to rectangular graves for the wealthier classes may be in part attributed to the increased use of coffins. Other changes in burial practices included the placement of funerary offerings further away from the body, eventually leading to multi-chambered tombs, one of the basic hallmarks of the later Egyptian culture.

Two new types of pottery appeared in the Naqada II Period: a rough utilitarian ware sometimes decorated with incised motifs, and a fancier ware with painted decorations or moulded handles. The rough ware was made with Nile silt and straw and after firing acquired a brownish-red colour. The fancier vessels were made of clay from the mouths of certain wadis and were tempered with sand instead of straw. When fired at low temperatures, the vessels turned pink and at higher temperatures they took on a greyish-green colour.

The painted motifs decorating the low-fired pink pots were either geometric or scenic (Plates 19, 20 and 21). The pots with geometric designs such as spirals, serrated lines and waves appeared early in the Naqada II Period (NIIb), while scenic designs appeared later (NIIc) and continued throughout the period. The scenic designs expressed the basic elements of the Egyptian world: desert and Nile animals, water, trees and boats. Male human figures were depicted, but only as minor elements

(a)

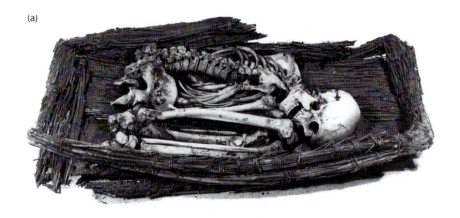

(b)

FIGURE 6.19 ◆ *Examples of an Egyptian basket (a) and wood coffin (b).*

within a larger scene; women, however, dominated some scenes, which may indicate that they occupied a privileged position. Female figurines of fired clay are also known from this period, but their significance, like the similarly portrayed females on pottery, remains a mystery.

FIGURE 6.20 ◆ *Grey-green ware with the wavy-handle lug (a) and the later decorative wavy design (b).*   Source: Courtesy of the Spurlock Museum, University of Illinois

The high temperature-fired vessels often took the form of the wavy-handled jars made famous by Petrie's classification system (Fig. 6.20). Wavy-handled vessels were first introduced into Egypt from Palestine; the form was then adopted and made locally. Wavy-handled jars were initially globular in shape with pronounced functional handles, but eventually evolved into a cylindrical shape with decorative, non-functional handles. The cylindrical jar with a painted rather than moulded wavy line around the middle became the most characteristic ceramic type of the succeeding Naqada III Period.

The Naqada II Period saw considerable advancement in stone working. Limestone, calcites and marble, as well as harder stone like basalt, gneiss and diorite, were used to make a variety of objects, including fine vessels resembling those previously fashioned out of clay (Fig. 6.21a and Plate 22). Given the skill and time needed to create one of these vessels, they probably were not for everyday use but were instead receptacles for exotic goods. Zoomorphic cosmetic palettes, a hallmark of Naqada I, had by this time become less common, the styles now leaning

(a)

(b)

FIGURE 6.21 ◆ *Naqada II stone vessels which, unlike earlier periods, are made from harder stones such as basalt.*

Sources: © Petrie Museum of Egyptian Archaeology, University College London

more to rhomboidal shapes often surmounted by two confronting animal heads (Fig. 6.22).

The disc-shaped mace heads of the Naqada I Period were replaced by pear-shaped mace heads (Fig. 6.23). Mystery still surrounds the adoption of the pear-shaped mace and how it became a symbol of power that lasted throughout Egyptian history: the motif can be seen in virtually all poses of the king smiting an enemy, from the beginning of Dynasty 1 to the end of the last dynasty (Fig. 6.24).

In the Naqada II Period the copper industry began to flourish. Copper artefacts such as blades, axes, bracelets and rings became more common, as did gold and silver objects (Fig. 6.25). We know nothing about which sector of society made the objects or of their smelting and casting processes. The production of metal tools, however, does indicate a level of hierarchical production previously not known in Egypt: first the ore was mined, then it had to be transported to the smelting area, then reduced and finally the objects were cast and the finished product was marketed. Even with its growing availability, copper was still deemed highly valuable, and tomb robbery was undertaken to recover it. Copper

FIGURE 6.22 ◆ *Two-headed palette with opposing effigies, a characteristic design of Naqada II.*

Source: © Brooklyn Museum of Art

FIGURE 6.23 ◆ *The pear-shaped mace replaced the earlier disc mace.*

Source: © Petrie Museum of Egyptian Archaeology, University College London

FIGURE 6.24 ◆ *Ptolemy XII, one of Egypt's last Pharaohs, smiting an enemy in the standard triumphant pose that dates back to the Dynasty 0 Narmer Palette.*

Source: Photograph by D. J. Brewer

(a) (b)

FIGURE 6.25 ◆ *Copper tools of the Naqada II Period: an adze (a) and an axe blade (b).*

Source: © Brooklyn Museum of Art

FIGURE 6.26 ◆ *An amulet shaped in the form of a bull's head.*
Source: © Brooklyn Museum of Art

was removed from graves frequently and with such precision that only a person witnessing the burial could have known exactly where to dig.

As in the previous period, the Naqada II people became increasingly fond of jewellery and other adornments (Plate 23), producing necklaces and bracelets with beads of stone, bone, ivory, shell, faïence and lapis lazuli. A popular amulet was one depicting a bull's head (Fig. 6.26). Female statues were also common in this period (Plate 24); interestingly they were three-dimensional versions of the same motifs that appeared on some painted ceramic vessels.

During Naqada I and early Naqada II times, Upper Egypt was home to many small, scattered villages, but as the seasonal rains diminished, drying up the desert borderlands, people began to migrate to the Valley. Eventually three large population centres evolved, located at important nodes for trade: Naqada, at the mouth of the Wadi Hammamat with its access to the Red Sea; Abydos, with its rich agricultural potential and proximity to the western oases; and Hierakonpolis, perfectly situated to command trade with Nubia.

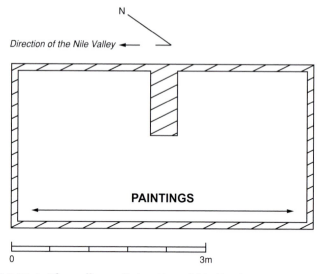

FIGURE 6.27 ◆ *The wall mural's location within Tomb 100.*

As the population expanded and a new social and economic order was evolving, so too was an ideological system, as we see in a tomb painting at Hierakonpolis. Tomb 100 was a rectangular brick structure measuring 5.85 by 2.85 metres (19.2 by 9.35 ft) with the floor at a depth of 1.5 metres (4.9 ft). The walls were mud brick covered by a layer of plaster elaborately decorated with Gerzean-style representations, the earliest known example of mural-type tomb painting in Egypt (Fig. 6.27 and Plate 30). Like the artistic renditions on ceramic vessels, the tomb decorations defy exact interpretation. The design was organised around a group of six immense boats that dominate the space. Around the boats, small scenes show hunting and warfare. The most interesting aspect of the painting is that it displays not only typical Naqada II pottery motifs but also motifs found on later Dynasty 0 ceremonial palettes.

Lower Egypt

The Omari culture

Postdating the Neolithic site of Merimde, where some of the earliest evidence for Egyptian domesticates has been recovered, the sites of

Omari, Ma'adi and Buto provide an interesting look at a developing Delta tradition. Omari (technically made up of two sites) was inhabited for roughly 200 years (4600–4400 BC), overlapping with the later occupations at Merimde and the early levels at Ma'adi. Omari, however, was not located where trade or contact with foreign groups might have regularly occurred. Rather, it seems to represent a typical village with a mixed hunting, fishing and farming subsistence. Interestingly, Omari pottery, although locally manufactured, possessed more Palestinian traits than did the pottery of nearby Merimde. Upper Egypt's influence can also be seen in burials where, although possessing few grave goods, the interred were oriented in the southern tradition (head south and body facing west). The inhabitants of Omari exploited the land to a greater extent than they did the river: the remains of domestic livestock and grains dominate the archaeological record, with fish and other Nile animals such as crocodile and hippo serving as a secondary source of food. Because Red Sea shells and galena from the Sinai have been recovered from the site, it is thought that some Omari people did venture beyond their immediate environment. While this alone does not prove Omarians engaged in long-distance travel and transport, the discovery of donkey remains, the earliest known in Egypt for this ancient beast of burden, strongly implies someone (if not the Omarians themselves) was moving goods over great distances at this time.

Ma'adi-Buto culture

The Ma'adi-Buto culture has only recently become part of Egypt's archaeological sequence. The large cemetery and settlement complex at Ma'adi and Buto (c.3400 BC) are the defining sites for the culture; hence the culture bears the sites' name. Apart from Ma'adi and Buto, approximately ten other sites have been identified as belonging to this culture, although most are much smaller in size (Fig. 6.28).

Excavations at Ma'adi found three types of settlement structures. The first is unique in Egypt: a subterranean house measuring 3 by 5 metres (9.84 by 16.4 ft) in area and up to 3 metres (9.84 ft) deep (Fig. 6.29). A succession of postholes along the house's walls suggests that there was an above-ground wooden structure that would have given the building a striking appearance. This house plan and the presence of hearths,

FIGURE 6.28 ◆ *The sites of Ma'adi, Buto and Heliopolis, core cultural areas of the Ma'adi-Buto culture of the Delta.*
Source: Redrawn by Brenda Coelho

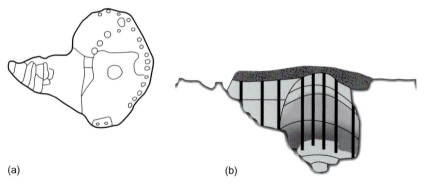

(a)   (b)

FIGURE 6.29 ◆ *The subterranean style house found at Ma'adi from above (a) and in profile (b). The closest known counterpart to this structure is found in Southwest Asia.*   Source: Brenda Coelho after Hoffman 1984, Fig. 54

half-buried jars and domestic debris imply that this house type was similar to those at Beersheba in southern Palestine.

The two other structure types found at Ma'adi are well attested in Egyptian history. The first is an oval hut accompanied by external stone line hearths and partly buried storage jars. The second is a rectangular construction with narrow trenches that held the stalks of plants; this was probably a fenced enclosure of some kind, possibly used to shelter animals.

FIGURE 6.30 ◆ *Ma'adian pottery vessels. Note the lugs and handles, which archaeologists believe helped facilitate their use in long-distance transport from the evolving cultures to the east.* *Source*: Photograph by D. J. Brewer

Pottery and lithics comprise the most dominant artefact classes at Ma'adi. Typical Ma'adian pottery vessels were globular with a flat base, a narrow neck and a flared rim; bottle shapes were also found (Fig. 6.30). Ma'adian vessels were rarely decorated but sometimes had marks incised after firing. Like the pot-marks of Upper Egypt, these incisions are poorly understood, but they may signify ownership, manufacturer or contents. Also found were examples of black-topped red ware, some clearly imports from Upper Egypt, but others exemplifying the Ma'adians' attempt to copy the southern style using local clay. The presence of Palestinian ceramic vessels, most importantly the wavy-handled vessels that were also copied by the Egyptians, suggests commercial links with that area.

Flint-working too was local but influenced by both Upper Egypt and Palestine. Stone vessels carved locally were made from soft stone such as limestone and alabaster, while vessels of hard stone such as basalt appear to be imports. Bone and ivory artefacts consisted mainly of needles and punches, although some combs imported from Upper Egypt were found.

Ma'adians were buried in oval pits, in a fetal position, wrapped in a mat or cloth. Originally, the bodies did not appear to be oriented in any particular directions but later they were positioned with the head to the south but facing east, not west, as in the south. What is most distinctive about the graves, however, is the near total absence of grave goods: at most, one or two pottery vessels might be included. No copper has been found in the burials, but often a Nile clam shell (*Apsatharia rubens*) has been recovered. At other sites, like Buto and Heliopolis, similar burial customs prevailed: burial pits were oval in shape, and bodies were placed in a fetal position, heads to south and facing east. Also evident at these sites was a tendency to copy Upper Egyptian material culture, particularly pottery and its associated Gerzian motifs, as well as the wavy-handled jars. Ma'adi is particularly important, however, because of its evidence for metalworking. While some speculation exists, Ma'adi may have possessed a smelting facility and have traded cast copper objects.

On the basis of all the evidence, Ma'adi appears to have been something of a commercial centre. Its position at the apex of the Delta makes it a perfect intersection for shipping goods between Palestine, Lower and Upper Egypt. Interestingly, Ma'adi seems to have had stronger ties to the Levant and Southwest Asia than to Upper Egypt. Perhaps the 250 km (155.3 miles) stretch of the Nile known as Middle Egypt, where no trace of Predynastic culture has been found, served as a buffer between the cultures. Further evidence for Ma'adi's role in trade are the remains of donkeys, the beast of burden and caravan animal of the period. The dominance of domestic plants and animals in archaeological excavations at Ma'adi suggests a near-total reliance on agriculture.

Although Ma'adi was a river port and the end point of a land route to the Levant, Buto, located in the northern Delta, may have been a seaport through which contacts with Sumer, Palestine and other cultures were made. Buto's location near the mouth of the Rosetta branch of the Nile and its proximity to the sea (then much closer to the site than today) placed it on a maritime route over which vast quantities of timber, oil, wine, minerals, pottery and other commodities could be imported and exported. Recent excavations at Buto have recovered clay cones similar to those used to decorate Uruk temples (*c*.3200 BC) in Mesopotamia, offering strong support to the claim of long-distance contacts via the sea (Fig. 6.31).

FIGURE 6.31 ◆ *Clay cone temple reconstruction, showing use of cones in decorative motif along a column.* Source: Loren Kirkwood after Roaf 1990

Based on the presence of Upper Egyptian artefacts, three phases have been identified in Ma'adian chronology. The earliest phase coincides with the last half of Naqada I and is best represented by the site of Ma'adi itself. The second phase is identified best with Heliopolis and the earliest levels of Buto, which date to middle Naqada II (e.g. between Naqada IIab and IIcd). The final phase, called Dynasty 0, is represented only at Buto.

In summary, by the end of Naqada II (*c.*3350 BC), Egyptian centres of political power such as Hierakonpolis, Naqada, Ma'adi and Buto had developed in both Upper and Lower Egypt, and local traditions began to merge – sometimes rapidly – into a definable national Egyptian character. Recent work at Abydos in Upper Egypt and Minshat Abu Omar in the Delta has revealed that, although Lower and Upper Egypt underwent separate stages of development, by late Naqada II Upper Egyptian culture characteristics were present in the eastern Delta. Excavations at Abydos suggest that at the end of the Naqada Period the cultural unification of

Upper and Lower Egypt had begun and may have culminated with the legendary unification of Egypt at Dynasty 0 (*c.*3050 BC). By this time, both Egypt's northern and southern sections exhibited what before had been a typically Upper Egyptian material culture, attesting to the gradual cultural domination of the north by the south.

By the end of the next period, called Naqada III, many of the features of the Dynastic Period are evident. Tombs at Abydos and evidence at Hierakonpolis indicate that these areas were ruled by local chieftain-kings who differentiated themselves from their subjects using symbols later assumed by the kings of Dynasty 1. Houses at Naqada were arranged along winding streets, indicating a city plan. Ivory tags with proto-hieroglyphs were in use and have been recovered from several sites, suggesting that, by the end of the Predynastic Period, writing was already established as a means of conveying rank, title and ownership. The cultural momentum established in the Naqada Period carried over into Dynasty I, finally culminating in the great era of Egyptian history, the Pyramid Age.

CHAPTER 7

The Late Predynastic: Naqada III and the quest for power

The concentration of power and wealth into the hands of fewer and fewer individuals, which intensified in the 200 years prior to the First Dynasty, typifies the late Predynastic culture. The different cultural identities of the Predynastic (Delta, Desert and Valley) – which in ancient times were as critically distinctive as being a Northerner or Southerner in the nineteenth-century United States – merged at this time to form one nation. How this transition occurred is not fully understood, but what does seem clear is that the operative word for this final period of Egyptian prehistory, called Naqada III, is consolidation.

Naqada III is divided into two parts, Naqada IIIa and IIIb, with the latter sometimes referred to as the Protodynastic or Dynasty 0. This latter period represents about 100 years and marks the transition between the old Predynastic order and the new Dynastic civilisation with a king, later to be known as Pharaoh, as its ruler. During this time we see the final step of consolidation: the population, its religion and its wealth all came under the control of a single ruler. Even artistic expression lost its provincial flavour and moved towards a national tradition.

Given the complexity of Naqada III culture, it is clear that Egypt's unification did not occur as the result of a single event or under the auspices of a single ruler. It was a long process in which climatic change, armed conflict, evolving agricultural efficiency and the development of new socio-political institutions were all interconnected and brought about the unified kingdom we see in the First Dynasty. Any discussion of Egypt's unification, therefore, must deal with these major elements of change: environmental, technological and social, and, perhaps most interesting, those changes brought about by foreign influences.

We have already seen that in Naqada II times (c.3500 BC) Hierakonpolis and Naqada had evolved into large population centres fully dependent on agriculture. At this time these centres were the largest communities in Upper Egypt, with smaller villages scattered around them as well as up and down the Nile. The Delta too had large and comparatively wealthy communities, such as Ma'adi, where goods were exchanged with Upper Egypt and the developing cultures to the east. In fact, other sites in the Delta such as Minshat Abu Omar and Buto indicate that by late Naqada II the Delta was part of a large trading network that extended east to Mesopotamia and west to the great desert oases. Slate palettes, ceramics and stone vases reminiscent of Upper Egyptian styles and with artistic motifs of eastern origin have been found at these Delta sites. Excavations at Buto suggest that it may have been an important port on an ancient maritime trade route over which vast amounts of timber, oils, wine and precious raw resources were carried (Fig. 7.1). By Naqada III, Egypt appears to have been an intricate partner in the region's international trade network.

Important environmental changes affected Egyptian life during this period. The first was the failure or discontinuance by about 3200 BC of the seasonal rains, which had been so important in fostering pastoral lifestyles in the regions west of the Nile. Slowly, through time, the rains became more unpredictable, eventually leading to the conditions of super-aridity experienced today. As a result, the desert dwellers had to choose between dying of thirst and hunger or abandoning their lifestyle for one more closely associated with the Nile. That some sort of migration occurred is evident at Hierakonpolis, Naqada, El-Kab and Adaima, where it appears that the region just beyond the Nile's black alluvium, which had been occupied by farming and herding villages in the Neolithic and Early Naqada Periods, became totally abandoned by Late Naqada times. The population apparently moved or resettled either in the vicinity of the already occupied Predynastic villages or on the available land near the towns.

FIGURE 7.1 ◆
Archaeological evidence
suggests that, by the late
Predynastic, Egypt had
entered into a broad trading
sphere that extended far to the
east, west and south over both
land and water routes.
Source: Redrawn by Brenda Coelho

This resettlement did not happen overnight but rather was a slow process extending over 100 or more years. Certainly there were times of abundant resources when newcomers to the Valley could be easily accommodated, but there were also periods of stress when Nile communities were not sufficiently provisioned to share grains and other foods with the newly arrived. The ominous prospect of more mouths to feed did have a positive outcome: with an increase in population came the need to feed that population, to organise resources better and to expand cultivable land; and because not everyone was directly involved in agricultural production, a socially acceptable system of exchange for services was established. In essence, the rudimentary constructs of a complex society were evolving.

The increase in population or more precisely in population density, although inspired by an environmental shift to aridity, was certainly a more complicated issue than presented here. For example, coupled with the loss of seasonal rains, a second environmental change occurred – a decline in the average Nile flood height. Scholars studying the Palermo Stone (Fig. 7.2), a Fifth Dynasty king list with records extending back into the Predynastic, suggest that Nile floods decreased in height

FIGURE 7.2 ✦ *The Palermo
Stone (under cross-polarised light),
a Dynasty 5 king list with entries
suggesting Nile flood heights.*
Source: Photograph by D. J. Brewer

about 0.7 metres (2.3 ft) from the First to Second Dynasty. Although it is
difficult to know if this phenomenon was in full progress by the late
Predynastic, any decline in flood height would probably have increased
the need to improve the efficiency of irrigation works and to expand the
storage and redistributive networks.

The regulation and expansion of irrigation networks has been considered by many archaeologists a hallmark in the genesis of civilisations.
Many scholars believed that, through irrigation and the related need to
organise labour and distribute water for the benefit of society, the initial
roots of civilisation began. The problem with this idea is that it was
initially applied indiscriminately to many developing cultures, and
subsequent research by archaeologists in these areas provided sufficient
evidence to question its veracity. In Mesopotamia, for example, irrigation
originated long before the nation-state. In applying these ideas to Egypt, a
second problem arises. Egyptian irrigation systems were never as extensive or as complex as those of Mesopotamia or China, and thus the need
for administrative organising was less of an issue. A famous study by

Karl Butzer showed that Egyptian irrigation networks revolved mainly around natural basins created by the convex topography of the Nile, and even then the reservoir water was used merely to even out the effects of the annual flood. Egypt's hydraulic networks were localised affairs, not extensive linear canals like their Mesopotamian counterparts; hence any political ramifications of irrigation would have been restricted to a small geographical area. Later Egyptian texts confirm this: the establishment and maintenance of local irrigation networks appear to have been the duty of local leaders or those aspiring to be such.

Nevertheless, irrigation technology was sensitive to political manipulation and was a focal point of community sentiment and organisation. By taking a lead role in its development and retaining a cut of the produce derived from such a community project, a new leader could pay for the services of a hydraulic engineer as well as reward other patrons for services rendered. The Scorpion Mace Head found at Hierakonpolis (Fig. 7.3) shows a king referred to as 'Scorpion' ceremonially opening an irrigation canal. As in modern building dedications, he is seen digging the first spade of dirt. Clearly this individual appreciated the fact that by sponsoring an irrigation project he owed and himself was owed debts and services – something important to any leader, particularly in times of political hardship.

To a greater extent than any other early complex culture, Egypt was a country of agriculturists, and Egypt's power and influence came from its agricultural productivity. Even though irrigation and agriculture were managed at the local level, the end results were legendary. Without question, even during Predynastic times Egypt was quite capable of producing abundant surpluses. That such surpluses were primary stimulants to the growth of states and civilisations is another favourite argument of historians and social evolutionists: surplus food had to be collected, stored and redistributed, and it freed part of the population to pursue craft production, religion and politics. These specialists in turn exchanged their services for food and gradually came to dominate society. However, this view implies that a bountiful agricultural economy necessarily leads to higher levels of social organisation such as civilisations and states, which is not always the case. Many food-producing societies rejected the notion that large stored surpluses were necessary and never developed into states. The basic impulse in these societies seems to have been to follow

(a)

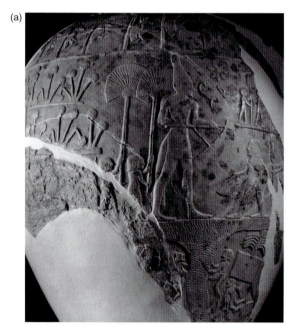

(b)

FIGURE 7.3 ◆ *The famous Scorpion Mace Head showing a Predynastic King Scorpion of Upper Egypt ceremonially opening an irrigation canal (diagramed below).*   Source: Werner Forman/Art Resources, NY. Ashmolean Museum, Oxford

the principle of least effort and keep just enough seed to propagate next season's crop and provide a small margin of safety.

For the collection and storage of surplus food to be a successful community venture required a degree of centralised decision making and an investment in the technology of food storage and redistribution. As early as Badarian times we see communal storage jars for grain, and these receptacles were enlarged and improved upon throughout the Predynastic Period: large buried ceramic vessels filled with wheat, barley and other agricultural products evolved into room-sized granaries and storage facilities.

Although by Naqada III times large population centres existed in both Upper and Lower Egypt, the Nile Valley remained rural in character, with the agricultural village as the predominant type of settlement. What did an ancient village or town look like? Unfortunately, it is very difficult to study this most common site type because, built of perishable materials such as reed mats and mud brick, they left little in the archaeological record. The earliest villages very likely originated in areas where environmental conditions allowed agriculturists to grow crops and sustain herd animals within an acceptable margin of risk. In Upper Egypt the best areas for sustaining villages were along the ancient river levees, which stood several metres above the surrounding plain and offered the village security from all but the highest floods. A village located on a levee gave the farmer direct access to adjacent cultivable land and the river, which was important for transportation, communication and rich fish resources. Such a location also offered proximity to the desert borderlands and the wild game that was attracted to those areas.

The ancient Egyptian hieroglyph for 'community' provides an additional clue to reconstructing an ancient Egyptian village. The sign (Fig. 7.4) used to designate an inhabited place is a circle bisected by crossed lines, suggesting perhaps that the archetypal village had a generally circular layout. Excavations of a Naqada I settlement at Abydos revealed a circular village plan about 30 metres (98.4 ft) in diameter. Work at Hememieh also revealed a circular or oval village configuration. A circular or oval settlement plan, with free-standing domiciles and separate outbuildings, was also evident in the lower levels of Predynastic Delta settlements such as Merimde, el-Omari and Ma'adi.

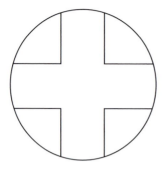

FIGURE 7.4 ◆ *The hieroglyph for village suggests a circular settlement pattern with cross-streets.*
Source: Redrawn by Brenda Coelho

By Naqada II, house type and community appearance changed. Mud brick became the favoured building material for houses, walls and other structures. Streets and alleys also appeared at this time, probably as a result of the architectural shift to rectangular or sharply angled structures. In addition, settlements with brick enclosure walls existed. Nevertheless, the community area itself seems to have retained its circular shape; on Late Predynastic and Early Dynastic slate palettes, settlements are shown as circles or ovals surrounded by stout, often buttressed, brick walls (Fig. 7.5).

FIGURE 7.5 ◆ *Artistic depictions of fortified villages from various votive palettes also reveal a circular shape for Egyptian villages.*
Source: Redrawn by Brenda Coelho

Towns probably evolved from villages in areas where the redistribution of goods was most effectively undertaken, such as along the terminal points of desert trade routes or adjacent to natural harbours along the river. Generally, towns had larger populations than villages and were internally more differentiated. That is, they served more private and public functions and offered a greater range of goods and services than did villages. Many of the earliest towns were also religious cult centres dedicated to a specific deity and thus filled a religious as well as a secular role.

Archaeological remains at Hierakonpolis suggest that a temple or shrine was an important feature of towns. The earliest temple there clearly dates to at least the Protodynastic Period (i.e. Naqada IIIb) and it is logical to infer that it provided a point of attraction for the local population and an arena for early politicians to organise a following. The Painted Tomb, a type of structure that could be afforded by only the most wealthy of persons, attests that such local leaders existed at Hierakonpolis at this time. In addition to its religious sector, Hierakonpolis also stood at an important juncture for trade with the growing Nubian cultures to the south.

Naqada also evolved into a town, probably because it sat at an important crossroad for trade with the east via the Wadi Hammamat. It has been suggested that contacts with cultures from Southwest Asia or their intermediaries occurred at Naqada or Hammamat. This speculation is based on a number of recovered artefacts with distinctive Asian motifs, depictions of boat types thought to represent Asian craft and the presence of raw materials that originated in Asia but have no observable trail of passage through the Delta or Lower Nile Valley.

The Delta also possessed a strongly rural population along the main river branches and elevated *geziras*. There too several large population centres such as Buto and Ma'adi gradually gained economic and possibly political control over an as yet poorly defined hinterland.

Life in these large population centres, like Hierakonpolis and Naqada in Upper Egypt and Ma'adi and Buto in Lower Egypt, had a much more cosmopolitan feel than did the evolving provincial towns. Excavations have not yet provided a reliable picture of how these cities might have looked, but they are thought to have been a conglomeration of residential areas located around various temple and administrative complexes. Memphis, the capital city founded, legend tells us, by the first king of

Egypt, was a massive community that through urban sprawl amalgamated a number of smaller semi-independent villages, creating a large population centre with distinctive neighbourhoods that were interspersed with fields and gardens.

The Upper Egyptian community of Thebes was little more than a small provincial town in the Early Dynastic but grew to become a capital city and religious centre. Although its greatest expansion occurred in the Middle and New Kingdom, post-dating the formative period by more than a thousand years, its evolution may be indicative of the growing Naqada III and Early Dynastic communities. Like Memphis, Thebes was, originally, a loosely linked series of settlements that coalesced into a larger population centre. It possessed a series of neighbourhoods that were socially mixed, with scribes, district officers, physicians, craftsmen, fishermen, potters, sandal-makers, gardeners and farmers all living in the same area. This mixture suggests that neighbourhoods were not stratified by profession, status or social class. The New Kingdom settlement at el-Amarna, a planned city created by King Akhenaten (c.1350 BC), also lacked any elite neighbourhoods or pattern of social or professional stratification, suggesting this mixing was a common feature of Egyptian towns and cities.

Although large settlements existed for long periods of time and grew in random fashion according to the needs of the inhabitants, they often expanded in the course of a single generation. Archaeological ground plans of such towns reveal a confusing labyrinth of narrow, oddly twisting alleys, passages, squares and courts, with little open space. In dense population areas, such as inside town walls, space was at a premium and houses grew upwards to two or possibly three storeys.

Excavation plans and modern reconstructions that provide an image of a clean and organised garden or park-like atmosphere for Egyptian settlements are far from accurate. Ancient Egyptian streets were not surfaced, and there was little proper sanitation and no system of drainage – sewage merely drained into the sub-soil. Domestic garbage was piled on rooftops, in alleys and in just about every available area. Refuse heaps were particularly large next to public wells and along the smaller winding alleys, thereby reducing access to many homes. As urban areas grew, these rubbish heaps were often levelled and even 'disinfected' by burning, and new houses and neighbourhoods were built on top of them.

The lifestyle of Egyptians who resided permanently in cities or towns differed in important ways from the lifestyle of villagers. Every Egyptian, however, was tied in some direct way to agricultural life; even bureaucrats had to deal with leasing land, accounting for harvests and taxation and redistribution of the proceeds. Town- and city-based governments also intervened in rural society through leasing land, tax collection, conscripted military and state labour forces, judiciary endeavours and other regulations that affected daily life.

It is quite certain from archaeological evidence that Naqada III Egyptians in some of the larger population centres were in contact with cultures to the east, south and west. Equally clear is that this interaction resulted in the borrowing of some fundamental concepts that in turn were instrumental in the evolution of Egypt's Pharaonic civilisation. The role of foreign contacts and their potential contribution has been seen as a prime mover to social complexity and nation-building. Early archaeologists even went so far as to postulate that a dynastic race of foreign origin had entered Egypt and taught the indigenous Nile dwellers the fundamentals of civilisation-building, although over the years this scenario has been proven inaccurate. That the Egyptians were impressed with the developing states of Mesopotamia, however, seems clear from their borrowing of eastern motifs, seen in early Egyptian art. The most classic example of these can be seen in several slate palettes (such as the Narmer and Delta Palettes), probably made to commemorate certain events (Fig. 7.6). These marvellous examples, however, represent the end point of a developmental sequence that dates back to earlier Predynastic periods. Examples of motifs on pottery, as well as the famous Gebel Arak knife (Fig. 7.7), show similar foreign motifs, albeit in less elaborate forms.

A critical development thought to have been borrowed from Mesopotamia is writing. Although all hieroglyphic symbols appear to be of Egyptian origin, the concept that a picture can convey a word and that words not readily understood through a picture can be conveyed phonetically by a series of pictures was until recently assumed to have originated in Mesopotamia (Box 7.1). Recent excavations at Abydos and along the Western Desert suggest, however, that Egyptian and Mesopotamian writing arose at the same time. The origin of writing in Egypt, like Mesopotamia, is linked to a growing national administration. Supervision and control of a burgeoning bureaucracy, the implementation of a tax

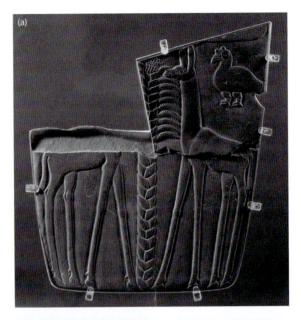

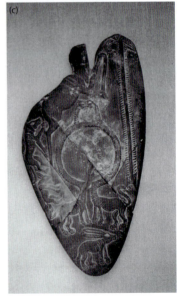

FIGURE 7.6 ◆ *Eastern motifs found on early votive palettes share a number of artistic styles with distinctive Mesopotamian influences, in particular animals with extended necks, which by the Protodynastic are shown intertwined.*

Sources: (a), (b) Werner Forman/Art Resources, NY. Ashmolean
Museum, Oxford; (c) photograph by David George

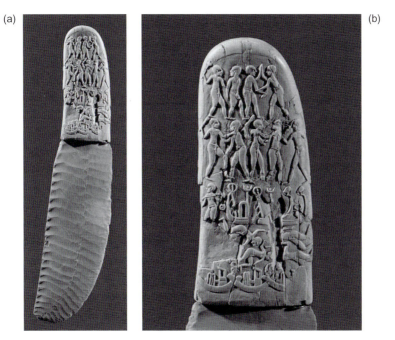

FIGURE 7.7 ◆ *The Gebel Arak knife is also thought to display foreign influences in the style of the high-prow (Mesopotamian?) boats locked in combat with local (Nile?) watercraft (bottom register of handle).*

Source: Erich Lessing/Art Resource, NY. Louvre, Paris

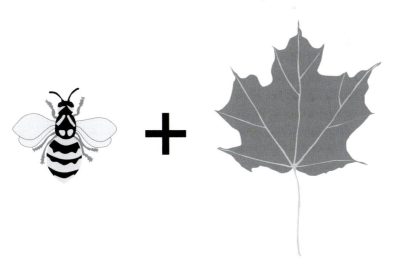

FIGURE 7.8 ◆ *Bee plus leaf equals belief, via the rebus principle.*

Source: Redrawn by Brenda Coelho

BOX 7.1 ◆ **Writing**

The Egyptian hieroglyphic script functioned according to the rebus principle, whereby symbols representing the sounds of actual objects were combined to form the pronunciation of abstract words that could not be conveyed by a picture. Thus, ancient Egyptian hieroglyphic symbols could represent a word (ideogram) or simply a sound within a word (phonogram), the latter being combined with other symbols to form more abstract words and sentences. For example, using the rebus principle with the English language, a picture of a bee could represent a bee or be a sound in a longer unrelated word such as belief. By using the rebus principle the picture of a bee combined with that of a leaf becomes belief (Fig. 7.8). Because this system is essentially phonetic, the signs employed to spell many Egyptian words bear no meaningful relationship to what they actually are, having been employed solely for their phonetic value.

system and tracking the import and export of trade goods required a means of accounting.

Writing aside, it seems undeniable that Egypt had foreign interactions and traded with other cultures. How then might this stimulus have helped Egypt coalesce into the earliest and most dynamic of early civilisations? Although we can find fault with each of the unilineal explanations (such as irrigation, agricultural surplus and trade) for the rise of Egyptian civilisation, when taken as a group with their complex interactions with one another, it is difficult to deny that these factors had a tremendous influence on Egyptian Predynastic culture. Environmental change, population shifts and advances in irrigation technology, grain storage and redistribution, as well as an influx of ideas from foreign lands – and other stimuli that we may never know – created a need for community organisation through a centralised government. Such a group or individual, either benignly or by force, organised the growing population so that it could be effectively directed to support public works and the administrative offices needed to run them. Thus, by Naqada III a number of powerful rulers controlled large areas along the Nile Valley.

Because deserts and seas border the Nile Valley, it was effectively isolated from the threat of foreign armies, but it was not so isolated as to prevent trade ships and caravans. The influx of foreign goods and services presented an opportunity for some local rulers to take a central role in cultural exchanges, eventually amassing tremendous wealth and the power that derives from such wealth. Gaining control over ports of entry eventually became a goal of some provincial rulers: control of trade meant wealth and power, which could be translated into political alliances.

By the middle of the Naqada III Period, many of the administrative offices needed to control the economic and agricultural aspects of the countryside were in place. In essence, all the elements of the dynastic civilisation had been achieved except the unification of Egypt under a single ruler. Iconographic evidence, such as the Gebel Arak Knife and the Narmer Palette, strongly suggests that this last step was a violent one, with an Upper Egyptian ruler forcibly annexing neighbouring territory to his own ancestral holdings until the entire Nile Valley fell under his control. While such conflicts undoubtedly occurred in some instances, the preponderance of archaeological evidence suggests a more peaceful annexation. Scholarly research suggests that unification was gained predominantly through economic means rather than physical combat. That is, through time, one finds Lower Egypt first emulating certain types of pottery and cultural traditions that historically belonged to Upper Egypt, then later fully adopting Upper Egyptian traditions and material goods. The process was not unlike that of the spread and adoption of American pop culture in even the most remote parts of the non-industrial world. It was a voluntary adoption that simply engulfed the Delta cultures to such a point that their own traditions were abandoned in favour of those from Upper Egypt. The people of the Nile Valley then accepted the new political regime and its ruler, ushering in the first great territorial nation. To be sure, some areas resisted and were forcibly annexed and, to a new king showing off his prowess, these are the episodes that would be chosen to be portrayed in commemorative objects.

The birth of any nation is a complex affair, but for Egypt it was even more so because no template for nation-building existed. Never before had such a large area been under the control of a single governing body or person. Because writing had yet to reach its full potential, oral history relayed the story of unification; like all stories, this history was made entertaining through the adventures of heroes, particularly the king, whose exploits in combat and other examples of male prowess were emphasised. These stories were eventually recorded in written form, parts of which have come down to us. It must also be remembered that these stories, in essence, served as propaganda designed to unify a people rather than to present accurate information. Beyond the territory brought under political control lay a vast and complex society that also had to adjust to this new order of government and accept the king as ruler. Through aggrandisement, the king took on the air of a god on earth and was accorded the respect and trust of the populace.

Ironically, and perhaps one reason for the quick adoption of the new order and its cultural longevity, is that life for the average person changed little from Predynastic to Dynastic times: farmers ploughed their fields, fishermen plied the waters of the Nile and craftsmen traded their products for sustenance. Certainly some changes were felt throughout the population: everyone had to deal with an increased number of bureaucratic offices and administrators, some being clearly redundant with previously existing offices; a local religion might have meshed with another belief system, but it remained comfortably distinct within its geographic area; and homage had to be paid to a ruler who was human but also a god.

The ruling class, on the other hand, probably experienced more profound changes. Some may have experienced purges, and shifts in policy requiring a realignment of loyalties undoubtedly occurred. Certainly everyone had to pay more taxes, but in general life was not unlike that of their Predynastic ancestors who also adjusted to numerous political shifts in an evolving social system. In a sense, life improved under the new order because an additional level of security came with centralised government: ills that befall large populations, such as famine, lawlessness and foreign intervention, were now mitigated at the national level rather than locally, offering much relief to the citizenry.

CHAPTER 8

In search of Egypt's first Pharaoh

Who was Egypt's first Pharaoh? Where did he come from? And how did he rise to power? As important as these questions are, we have no contemporary documents or artefacts to answer them. Whether archaeologists simply have not found the evidence or no documents commemorating the event were ever created is difficult to say. Thus, to understand who this man was and what he accomplished, we must look to an early Egyptian legend.

In this legend, as in other early references to Egypt's first king, you will not find the word Pharaoh, which comes from the Egyptian term *Per aa* or 'great house', referring to the king's palace. Like modern references to the White House or Number 10 Downing Street, 'Pharaoh' was used as a polite, indirect referent to the king, but it did not come into popular use until the New Kingdom. During the Early Dynastic the holder of the office was simply referred to as king and was addressed as 'his majesty'.

According to ancient Egyptian tradition, Menes, King of Upper Egypt, who founded the First Dynasty and built the capital city of Memphis, is credited with being the unifier of the nation.

> . . . *the first royal house numbers eight kings, the first of whom Menes of This reigned for 62 years. He was carried off by a hippopotamus and perished.*

> [Africanus (Manetho Fr. 60)]

The King called [Menes] reigned for 60 years. He made a foreign
expedition and won renown but was carried off by a hippopotamus.

[Eusebius (Manetho Fr. 7)]

The priests told me that Menes was the first king of Egypt and that first
he separated Memphis from the Nile by a dam . . . Then, when this first
king [Menes] had made what he thus cut off to be dry land, he first
founded in it that city which is now called Memphis.

[Herodotus II:99]

These written accounts of Menes' accomplishments, however, date thousands of years after his death, by which time he had been transformed into a cult hero whose life and accomplishments were embellished with semi-mythical anecdotes. In fact, it is difficult to prove if Menes actually existed and his accomplishments were real, or if he was simply a fable and his exploits were the work of other individuals now lost to history. Without contemporary written records we can only examine this quasi-historical figure and his accomplishments using archaeological data, which is, unfortunately, better suited to interpret cultural changes across generations than the specific accomplishments of an individual. Nevertheless, the search for Menes has deep relevance to the origins of Egypt and to the relationship between history and prehistory.

Perhaps the easiest question to answer is where Menes or his real-life counterpart came from. According to several king lists, the rulers of the first two dynasties came from the Thinite nome of Upper Egypt, identified in modern times as the area around Abydos; in fact the tombs of the First Dynasty kings are located at Abydos, as are the tombs or graves of the royal entourage. Considerable evidence of 'a royal presence' at Hierakonpolis has also been recovered, which indicates it too held an important role in Late Predynastic and Early Dynastic times. It has been suggested that Hierakonpolis, located 175 km (109 miles) south of Abydos, served as the political seat of government and Abydos as a religious centre, but the true relationship between Abydos and Hierakonpolis remains in question. Possibilities include: Hierakonpolis and Abydos served separate secular and religious roles; Hierakonpolis was the original capital and the government moved downstream to Abydos in the course of assimilating northerly territories; or the rulers of Abydos subjugated Hierakonpolis. It could even be that Abydos and

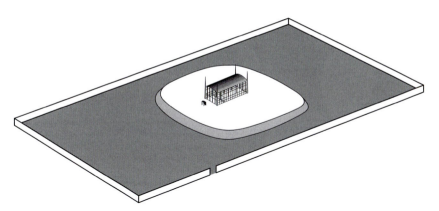

FIGURE 8.1 ◆ *The Hierakonpolis shrine as it may have appeared in the Late Predynastic.* Source: After Lehner, Mark, *The Complete Pyramids* (Thames and Hudson, 1997). Redrawn by Loren Kirkwood

Hierakonpolis forged an alliance and together campaigned against the north.

At Hierakonpolis a temple or shrine dating to late Naqada II (Naqada IId) provides significant evidence of centralised political leadership in the area. At the end of the Naqada II Period there appears to be a hiatus in activity at the temple, with a purposeful destruction or tear down of the structure. By Naqada III times a new temple, constructed on the same site, was in use. It consisted of a courtyard and several outbuildings. The buildings were made of woven matting held up by wooden poles and bundled straw pillars (Fig. 8.1). A raised dais offered a platform for the local ruler to watch the activities in the courtyard. This centre, whether religious, secular or both, very likely served as a point of organisation and dissemination of power.

At Abydos, the royal cemetery seems to have developed as an extension of the earlier Naqada burial ground. The cemetery contains many typical Predynastic graves, dating from the Naqada I and II Periods, but also brick-lined tombs of the Naqada III Period, some elaborately constructed with multiple rooms (Fig. 8.2). Such evidence suggests that powerful individuals, perhaps the forerunners to the First Dynasty kings, were buried in these sepulchres.

The contents of the Abydos tombs were remarkable even after repeated looting over the years. Materials recovered include ceramics, both locally made and imported, and simple text inscriptions, among

---

BOX 8.1 ◆ Hierakonpolis temple mound (see Fig. 8.1)

It is possibly at the late Naqada temple mound of Hierakonpolis that the basic concepts of Egypt's divine kingship appear for the first time. The circular mound was contained by a revetment or retaining wall measuring nearly 50 metres (165 ft) across with a sloped angle of 45°. Its original height is not known because the mound was probably cut down for building later structures. A temple was built around the mound, probably near the beginning of the First Dynasty. Atop the mound was a chapel, which, as the highest point of elevation in the area, would have offered a ruler a commanding view of his subjects. Just such a shrine is depicted on commemorative objects such as the Narmer Mace Head, recovered from the same deposit as the famous Narmer Palette.

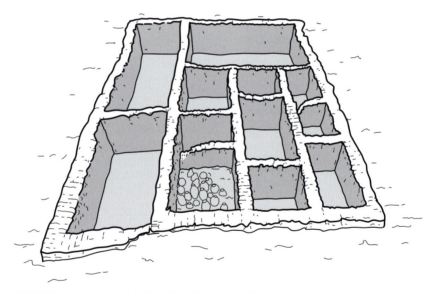

FIGURE 8.2 ◆ *A multi-chambered tomb at Abydos.*

Source: Redrawn by Loren Kirkwood

which were *serekhs*, a panelled rectangle surrounding the king's name (Fig. 8.3).

Serekh was an Egyptian word that meant 'to make known'. The *serekh* design, it is thought, was based on an architectural feature intimately linked with royalty, the niched façade. Like other innovations of this

FIGURE 8.3 ◆ *The Serekh of King Djet (Wadji), third ruler of Dynasty 1.*

Source: Réunion des Musées Nationaux/Art Resources, NY.
Louvre, Paris

period (e.g. cylinder seals, artistic representations of animals), the niched façade is associated with the evolving cultures of the Mesopotamian region. The design of the niched façade was an attempt to reproduce in brick what had previously been constructed out of reed mats and bundles. The reed screens used as walls were held upright by bundled reeds, which projected outwards beyond the mat screens, giving the façade a panelled appearance, which was later stylistically represented in stone. Niching can be seen on the Second Dynasty mortuary complex of Khasekhemui (Fig. 8.4) and most dramatically on the wall surrounding the Dynasty III Step Pyramid of Djoser. This is the feature that is portrayed on the *serekh*, intimating that the name contained within the niched panel is royal.

From *serekh*s and king lists we know the succession of Early Dynastic rulers, as well as some of the important events that occurred during their respective reigns. The king lists are particularly important because they provide a year-by-year accounting of important events that occurred during a given king's rule (Fig. 8.5). When comparing names across the different king lists, however, some problems arise. First, because the extant sources used to compile our current succession of kings are based on ancient copies of earlier lists, names, duration of reigns and even

(a)

(b)

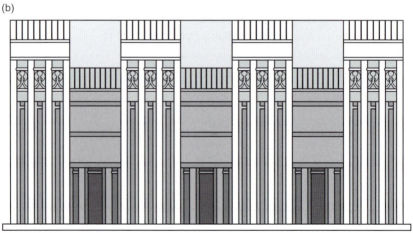

FIGURE 8.4 ◆ *Façade niching along the wall of the ancient Fort of Khasekhemui (a) and diagrammed to show detail (b).*

Sources: (a) © Jeremy Geller; (b) Redrawn by Loren Kirkwood

FIGURE 8.5 ◆ *The king list of the Mortuary Temple of King Seti I, father of the great King Ramesses.* Source: Erich Lessing/Art Resource, NY. Temple Seti I, Abydos

spellings of the same name differ. Second, each king had five separate names. We recognise most kings by their Horus name (see p. 149), but for the early dynasties the lists use the *nsw*-name, which complicates identifications. For example, King Den's *nsw* name was Sempti, but through confusion of the hieroglyphs it is listed as Septi in the Abydos list, and his Greek name, Usaphais, is used in Manetho's king list. Despite these difficulties, by comparing lists and using additional textual evidence recovered from archaeological excavations, a reasonable list of early kings' names exists.

Two sources of corroborative evidence that help clarify the identity and succession of the early rulers are cylinder seals and engraved tags. Cylinder seals (Fig. 8.6) first appeared in Egypt in Naqada II as imports from Mesopotamia. These were copied by the Egyptians, who like their eastern neighbours used them as a means of labelling mud seals and stoppers on pottery jars. One seal dated to about 3000 BC lists the first five kings of Egypt in sequential order (Fig. 8.7).

Engraved tags of ivory, bone or ebony provide additional information (Fig. 8.8). These were generally used for everyday purposes such as demonstrating possession of funerary equipment or listing the number of

(a)

(b)

FIGURE 8.6 ◆ *A Predynastic cylinder seal carved from a hippo tusk. The cylinder was rolled across wet clay, leaving its impression as a signature of ownership, contents or manufacturer (b).*

Source: © Petrie Museum of Egyptian Archaeology, University College London

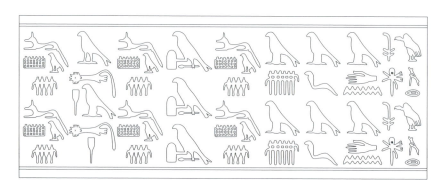

FIGURE 8.7 ◆ *Cylinder seal impression listing first five kings of Dynasty 1.*

Source: After Spencer, A. J., *Early Egypt: The Rise of Civilisation in the Nile Valley*, courtesy of the Trustees of the British Museum. Redrawn by Brenda Coelho

(a)

(b)

FIGURE 8.8 ◆ *(a) An ivory label from one of King Den's sandals; (b) an accurate recreation of a label of King Aha with the* mn *glyph (upper right), suggesting he might be Menes, first ruler of Egypt.*

Sources: (a) © Brooklyn Museum of Art; (b) After Spencer, A. J. (see p. 132)

beads on a necklace, but they sometimes chronicled important events in the reign of a king. In fact, to date, the earliest corpus of Egyptian writing known to us comes from a group of labels recovered from a wealthy Predynastic Naqada tomb. By analysing the *serekhs* and tags, archaeologists have identified the tombs thought to belong to Kings Aha, Iry-Hor, Ka and Narmer. Seal impressions and fragments of inscribed pottery have further substantiated the identity of these rulers. Narmer, of course, is well known from the slate palette found at Hierakonpolis; Ka and Iry-Hor are less well known, and some controversy does exist as to whether Iry-Hor was indeed a ruler's name or a simple reference to the royal treasury. Nevertheless, the distribution of burials at Abydos and the evolution of the tombs' complexity provide a clear sign of continuity between the Late Predynastic and Early Dynastic rulers.

The analysis of archaeological and textual sources leaves us with little doubt that Predynastic leaders ruled Egypt, or parts of Egypt, several generations before the legendary Menes and the First Dynasty. It is also clear that some of the events included in these king lists took place prior to the use of writing and must have been passed down orally through several generations before finally being recorded.

How does Menes emerge from this picture? Let us consider the evidence that has survived from the actual period of unification rather than what was written many generations after the events occurred. Beginning in the late Naqada III Period, the king's name is found incised or painted on pottery within the rectangular *serekh*. While some *serekhs* held the king's Horus name (the name commonly used to identify the king), some *serekhs* were left empty and others were inscribed with yet untranslated words, perhaps identifying the owner, contents or manufacturer of the vessel. The typological classification of these ceramics from the Naqada III Period to the First Dynasty has allowed scholars to place the *serekhs* – and therefore the king's names – in chronological order (Fig. 8.9).

The earliest *serekhs* lacked inscriptions but were often surmounted by double falcons. These were followed by *serekhs* that featured the rulers Ka and Narmer, and finally a third group of *serekhs* featured Aha, establishing a sequence of rulers that is corroborated by archaeological excavations at Abydos, where the tombs of most of these leaders reside.

Researchers seeking to identify Menes have equated him, for one reason or another, with each of these early kings, even suggesting that

FIGURE 8.9 ◆ *Serekhs in chronological order (top to bottom).*

Source: Brenda Coelho after Kaiser and Dryer 1982, Ab. 14

one man was called Menes-Narmer-Scorpion. Figure 8.8b is a sketch of an ivory label from an oil jar with a record of an event in the reign of King Aha, whose *serekh* appears in the top line (second glyph from right). What is interesting is that the top register also contains the hieroglyph *mn* (right of *serekh*), linking, many believe, Aha to Menes. The search for Menes would end here were it not for the work of others who see the same *mn* sign used as a designate for several kings. Some scholars even suggest that *mn*, which in Egyptian meant 'to ensure' or 'make permanent', was actually an idiomatic expression that scribes used to designate any individual on whose behalf some ritual was undertaken but whose name they could not read or translate. Thus 'Menes' would refer to 'King what's his name' or 'King so-and-so'.

Whether Menes was a mythical figure or a real person who went by another name we may never know. Menes was said to have established a capital at This (near Abydos) and to have founded the city of Memphis. Three kings, Ka, Narmer and Aha, could lay claim to these accomplishments, because each has a tomb at Abydos and their names are all inscribed on material deriving from cemeteries in the Memphite region. However, two ceramic jars bearing Ka's *serekh* have been recovered from graves at Helwan, apparently indicating that the city of Memphis, which the Helwan necropolis served, was already in existence by his reign. During Aha's reign the first tombs were built in the cemetery at Saqqara, the necropolis for Dynasty II kings. This, combined with the establishment of the great Memphite necropolis and the existence of the term *mn* on the Aha labels, serves to explain the presence of this king at the head of the surviving king lists.

However, this still does not answer the question of who unified Egypt and how. Legend describes Menes as the first human ruler of Egypt (as opposed to gods ruling on earth) and founder of Memphis, but it does not identify him as the one who actually united the country. Ka might be given credit if not for founding Memphis then at least for establishing a capital at This – but did he rule over a unified Egypt, as did Narmer and Aha? It is clear from the iconography on the Narmer Palette that Narmer claimed to reign over a unified country (Fig. 8.10). This constitutes the first piece of written evidence of a southern ruler's conquest of the north.

The palette honours the exploits of Narmer and presumably his prowess in combat. At the top on either side of the palette within the

FIGURE 8.10 ◆ *The Narmer Palette, the earliest known text proclaiming unification: (a) the obverse side.*

Source: Jean Vertut 'L'art de l'ancienne Egypte' – Citadelles & Mazenod, Paris

serekh is King Narmer's name, framed on both sides by the benevolent cow goddess, Bat. On the obverse side, Narmer is shown wearing the *deshret*, the red crown of the Delta cities of Buto and Sais, later to become the characteristic headgear of the Pharaoh as king of Lower Egypt (Fig. 8.10b). The king is preceded by his priest and four standard-bearers carrying fetishes; his sandal-bearer and foot washer brings up the rear of the precession. His entourage inspects rows of corpses with bound arms and severed heads. The place of slaughter is identified from the glyphs above the bodies as a Delta city, probably Buto. The central register of

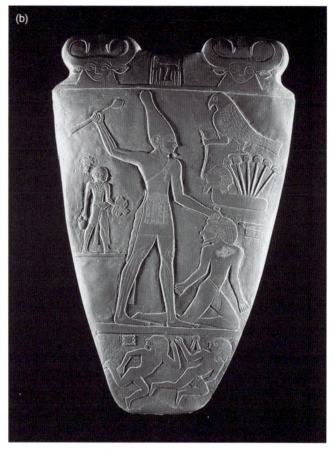

FIGURE 8.10 ◆ *(continued) (b) The reverse side of the Narmer Palett.*

Source: Werner Forman/Art Resources, NY. Egyptian Museum Cairo

this highly organised design shows a circular depression, around which are two four-legged creatures with intertwined serpent-like necks. This foreign-inspired character has been interpreted as a theme of union, Narmer being responsible for joining the two into one. At the bottom of the palette the king, symbolised as a 'strong bull', breaks down a fortified township and tramples a foreigner, identified as a Delta dweller or perhaps a Libyan.

The reverse side of the palette (Fig. 8.10a) shows Narmer, accompanied by his sandal-bearer, wearing the white crown, the *hedjet*, which was to become the emblematic headgear of the Pharaoh as King of Upper

BOX 8.2 ◆ Art and the Narmer Palette

The Narmer Palette serves as the first example in Egyptian art of arranging a work in organised parallel registers (see Fig. 8.10). Prior to this example, figures were scattered without any apparent order across the surface of the medium. The Narmer Palette shows the first steps towards scale and organisation. Egyptian art does not read right to left or left to right – it reads from larger to smaller, the larger figures being the most important, the smaller subsidiary figures and scenes used as background or additional information. The large main figures of the palette show the king in a controlled pose of power, an artistic canon that would carry through the next 3,000 years. The smaller figures in the subsidiary palette scenes, however, provide a more dynamic picture of movement and action – again a trait that would carry over to the Dynastic Period.

The motifs displayed on the palette also appear transitional in that they have a distinctive Egyptian style but retain vestiges of older Mesopotamian influences.

Egypt. The king is shown clubbing a submissive enemy with a pear-shaped mace in a pose that becomes engrained in Dynastic art and can be found on commemorative works for the next three millennia (see also Fig. 6.24). Above the victim are hieroglyphic symbols that read 'domain of the harpoon', which in later periods is a reference to a district of the Delta. Another reference to the Delta can be found above the hieroglyphs where the head of a defeated enemy is situated within a thicket of six papyrus plants. A falcon leads the tethered enemy by the nose, as one would lead a tamed bull. The message that the king has subdued the enemy seems quite clear. Because Narmer appears here as the King of both Upper and Lower Egypt, he has been equated with the semi-legendary Menes.

Is our question answered? Can we identify Menes as Narmer, the first ruler of a unified Egypt (Fig. 8.11)? The recent discovery of an engraved tag contemporary with the Narmer Palette and relaying a similar message of conquest over a delta (or Asiatic) enemy would seem to solidify Narmer as Mendes, but evidence to the contrary has also surfaced. A *serekh* of Ka

FIGURE 8.11 ◆ *Bust identified by Petrie as being that of King Narmer.*

Source: © Petrie Museum of Egyptian Archaeology, University College London

found on a cylinder seal from the site of Tarkhan and other inscriptions from Abydos refer to revenue received by the royal treasury, suggesting that a functioning centralised economy existed prior to Narmer's reign. There are even some who argue that a shadowy earlier figure known as King Scorpion also ruled a united Egypt.

King Scorpion, who preceded Ka and Narmer, is poorly known in Egyptian history. The famous Scorpion Mace Head from Naqada III levels at Hierakonpolis shows a king, identified as Scorpion, wearing the white crown of Upper Egypt standing triumphantly over a canal with a hoe in hand, probably commemorating the success of an irrigation project (see Fig. 7.3). Plants characteristic of Lower Egypt can also be seen. The reverse side of the mace head is unfortunately destroyed, but some scholars believe it may have shown the king wearing the red crown of Lower Egypt, signifying a claim to rule all of Egypt. Recent discoveries at Abydos, however, suggest that the scorpion sign found on this piece is a title rather than a name, and thus King Scorpion may not be the proper designation for the individual. Nevertheless, his real-life counterpart, whoever he might have been, may have ruled in some sense over parts of both Upper and Lower Egypt

If so, then what do we make of the Narmer Palette, where clearly the message is that King Narmer has conquered districts of the Delta and claims rulership of both north and south? What about the Scorpion Mace Head or Aha's accomplishments in establishing the Memphite necropolis?

It may be that the Narmer Palette, like the Scorpion Mace Head and other commemorative objects, portray victorious events. Numerous Predynastic palettes exist, all with a central theme of victory over a natural impediment or human enemy. But prior to Naqada III there is no evidence that actual kings existed. From Late Naqada II (Naqada IIcd) onwards, it is possible that powerful, small-scale kings were occasionally able to bring together large populations and territory under their control. The territory and communities they influenced probably waxed and waned through the generations, until finally individuals with sufficient power and charisma brought greater amounts of territory under their control and commemorated these events symbolically through the artefacts we have recovered. That is, they were able to combine actual rulership with the symbols of rulership that we recognise today as royal symbols of the Pharaoh.

From this point of view, the Narmer Palette perpetuates a culturally accepted scenario and, therefore, should perhaps be regarded as a monument commemorating an achieved state of unity rather than depicting the process of unification itself. The Narmer Palette perhaps simply provides evidence of an earlier example of smiting Lower Egypt, a feat repeated by Khasekhemui, who two centuries later had to put down civil unrest in the Delta and reunify Egypt. In other words, it may simply be the first known example of a violent means of expressing a process that had already taken place in earlier times. The assimilation of the Delta into southern Naqada culture may have been repeated at several historical junctions but was finally immortalised by the Narmer Palette.

Thus Menes probably never existed, at least as the individual responsible for all the attributed feats. Rather he is most likely a compilation of real-life individuals whose deeds were recorded through oral tradition

---

BOX 8.3 ◆ The hippo in Egypt

The hippopotamus held a significant place in Egyptian mythology as a symbol of danger. A common Old Kingdom tomb relief shows the deceased harpooning a hippo, demonstrating his prowess over the strength of the animal and, symbolically, his ability to control chaos. In a real sense the hippo was the personification of danger. Contrary to popular belief, the hippo can be quite aggressive in the water and Egyptians were always wary of its presence. If it became entangled in the large fishnets used by the Nile fishermen, it could not only destroy the net and damage the boat but drown the boat's occupants as well. Hippos were also known to ravage crops. In short, the hippo's reputation for danger was well deserved.

---

and identified as the work of a single person, thereby creating a central hero figure for Egypt's unification. Like the personalities of the Bible, Menes was part fiction, part truth, and the years have masked the borderline, creating a legend of unification. Even his death is apocryphal, having been devoured and carried away by a hippopotamus, the fitting end to a ruler of the Nile.

How then did unification occur? Most likely it was a slow process stimulated by economic growth. The south, with its unique cultural icons and dynamic political forces, slowly assimilated northern territories: new grazing and agricultural lands were needed and exotic trade goods were in high demand, and the Delta offered an opportunity to fulfil these needs. At first, Upper Egyptian styles were voluntarily accepted, even copied, by Lower Egyptian craftsmen, as were other aspects of the culture. Territory was plentiful and absorbed into Upper Egyptian estates without much fanfare, but as Upper Egypt became more centrally controlled and as population centres began to emerge in the Delta and exert their own influence over their immediate surroundings, trade and political and economic competition resulted. Because these Delta centres of commerce functioned well both politically and economically, it seems certain that at least some of them had to be forcibly pacified and annexed by Upper Egypt (sometimes more than once). The very rendering of names of the early kings relate an era of violence: Aha meant 'fighter'; Wadji, 'cobra'; Djer, 'palisade'; and Dewen, 'the spearer'. Even Narmer, which means 'mean (or nasty) catfish', represents a prolific and aggressive Nile predator.

The First Dynasty and the rise of the first king do not represent the first time Egypt had coalesced into a large territorial nation, but rather the first time the union held together for a long enough period of time to establish a national identity. Along with this national union came a vibrant economy, religious institutions and more centralised government. The union later failed on more than one occasion and the country had to be reunited: the troubles of the late Second Dynasty under Khasekhemui or at the end of Dynasty 6 (2181 BC) when the Old Kingdom totally collapsed serve as examples. However, a united Egypt with a strong central government was linked to economic prosperity and security from famine and foreign threats, and unity became the goal of all Egypt's later kings and an integral part of cultural identity for the peasantry. To be an Egyptian meant something, and early Egyptians felt an air of superiority to all their neighbours.

CHAPTER 9

Early Dynastic life

A lthough it seems obvious, given the size of the Egyptian population and the different tasks that were being performed, that a multi-tiered society existed by Dynasty 1, specifics about its make-up and various levels are difficult to determine. The population expansion that began in the Naqada Period not only set the stage for the rise of cities and the expansion of political ties into the Delta, Palestine and beyond, but created a large labour force as well. Readily available labour combined with the fertility of the Nile Valley enabled Egypt to produce mass surpluses of food. These agricultural surpluses in turn allowed other segments of society to engage and specialise in non-agricultural pursuits such as stone working, pottery manufacture and art.

Through evidence from burials, we can distinguish three levels of Early Dynastic society: nobles and high officials, mid-level bureaucrats and artisans, and the peasantry. The burials of nobility were located near the royal burials at Saqqara and Abydos; their graves, as with those of royal family members and high court officials, were all equipped with the furniture necessary for a luxurious afterlife. Across the river from Saqqara at Helwan, the tombs of middle-class, lesser nobles and officials of the court and government were located. They were much smaller and with fewer furnishings than the tombs of nobility, although they too reflect a high standard of living. The artisan class is represented in the tombs that surround the graves of the kings, nobles and high officials. Here again the tombs are smaller than those of nobles, high officials and working bureaucrats, but they were still furnished with food, drink and the equipment necessary to ply their craft in the afterlife. Peasants were interred much like their Predynastic ancestors, in shallow oval graves, but by the end of Dynasty 2 even the peasantry were buried with more goods and furnishings, although they pale in comparison with those of higher social standing.

To be sure, in newly united Egypt, life was in many ways similar to life in the Predynastic, but in many significant ways it was different. Because written records of the time are limited in scope, focusing primarily on enumerating goods, services and royal exploits, we must use alternative, more speculative means of investigating life in the Early Dynastic Period. For example, by employing anthropological methodology, archaeologists can offer some generalisations about Early Dynastic social structure, but as yet we cannot prove these assertions to be completely accurate. For instance, we can extrapolate back from the Old Kingdom and postulate about some aspects of earlier dynasties. A culture that is known to be patrilineal in historical times, for example, is likely to have been patrilineal in its Late Prehistoric Period. Such cultural practices tend to be very resilient to change and to continue even under the most extreme circumstances. Therefore, many well-established hallmarks of later Egyptian society very likely extend back into the Late Prehistoric Period. Over the millennia, they evolved in complicated ways, but the basic building blocks probably remained intact.

The central government

During the first three dynasties, often called the Early Dynastic Period, the institution of kingship was already central to the Egyptian state and government. Although the office can be traced to the Protodynastic, Egyptians believed the line of kings extended back into prehistory, to a time when gods lived on Earth. Even in the First Dynasty the king was considered a descendant and incarnation of the god Horus, who succeeded his father Osiris in an unbroken chain of related rulers. The symbolic emblems of office included a special kilt (the *shendty*), a sceptre, a crook and flail, as well as various crowns, most notably the white crown of Upper Egypt and the red crown of the Delta.

The complex character of Early Dynastic kings was expressed in their titles, which included three names that served to reinforce the king's role as ruler of the two lands, Upper and Lower Egypt. Even at this early

BOX 9.1 ◆ The Early Dynastic defined

The Early Dynastic generally refers to Dynasties 1 and 2, but recently scholars have included Dynasty 3 within this period. From this perspective, Dynasty 3 is seen as the culmination of the formation process of the Egyptian state government and its monuments. Scholars viewing Dynasty 3 as part of the Old Kingdom point to the step pyramid as the indicator that social progress in Egypt had entered a new age. As in other periods of transformation (e.g. Naqada I to Naqada II), these labels are being imposed on a fluid process and therefore should be recognised as simply markers for grouping the various dynasties into scholarly workable packages. This book treats Dynasty 3 as part of the formative period but only in the sense of bringing the aspects of the long Prehistoric Period to its appropriate (and logical) end.

BOX 9.2 ◆ Osiris

One of the most significant functions of Egyptian ritual and myth was the reinforcement and protection of both the office and body of the king, and the most important myth associated with kingship was the Osiris myth, elements of which probably date to the Predynastic with the most elaborate version coming from the second-century AD writings of Plutarch. The focus of the myth, regardless of version, was to associate the living king with the god Horus and his deceased predecessor and father Osiris. In this way, each king of Egypt was incorporated into a mythological descent from the time of the gods. The myth also stressed filial piety and obligations of a son to his father.

The myth of Osiris

Osiris is described as the great-grandson of Re, grandson of Shu, and first son of Geb and Nut. In due course he succeeded his father as king in Egypt, marrying his sister Isis. Osiris's earthly rule was just and wise. He organised his people's agricultural, religious and secular life, and he also concerned himself with peaceful foreign conquest, ably assisted by

Isis, his Vizier Thoth, and the officials Anubis and Wepwawet. This happy state of affairs was to be destroyed by Seth, the younger brother of Osiris, who was jealous of Osiris's power and prestige and coveted the throne for himself. When Osiris returned to Egypt from travels abroad, Seth invited him to a banquet at which 72 accomplices were also present. During the festivities a beautifully decorated casket was brought into the hall and much admired by everyone. Seth promised that the casket would be given to the person who fit inside it perfectly. Because the casket had been made to the measurements of Osiris, when it was his turn to get inside, it was an exact fit. Seth and his followers immediately closed the lid and fastened it securely. The casket was cast into the Nile in the hope that it would travel to the sea and be lost forever. The casket washed ashore near the city of Byblos on the Syrian coast close to the base of a young tamarisk tree, which grew and enclosed the casket within its trunk. The tree grew to be a fine specimen and was chopped down and made into a column to support the roof in the King of Byblos's palace.

Meanwhile, in Egypt, Isis had heard what Seth had done to her husband and in great distress she set out to find him. Eventually she came to Byblos and succeeded in having the column removed, and retrieved the casket and took it back to Egypt, where she hid it in the marshes of the Delta. Seth discovered it and attempted to destroy his brother's body permanently by cutting it up into 14 pieces, which he distributed throughout Egypt. Isis soon became aware of this outrage and travelled all over the country searching for the pieces of the body. Her sister Nephthys, the wife of Seth, did not condone these actions and helped her in her search. Egyptian references differ here. Some say that all 14 pieces were recovered. Other sources, such as Plutarch, state that all parts were recovered expect the phallus, which had been devoured by fish. Isis with her magical powers then had to create a substitute. According to certain texts Isis and Nephthys buried each part of the body in the place where they found it (which would explain the number of sites in Egypt associated with the burial of Osiris). In other versions Isis collected the body parts, rejoined them to create a mummy and performed the rites, which gave the dead Osiris eternal life. In Plutarch's account, Isis had already given birth to her son Horus, but other sources state that she conceived the child from her husband's dead body.

ANCIENT EGYPT: THE ORIGINS

The resurrected Osiris had no further part to play on Earth, and as the immortal dead king he became the ruler of the dead. Although Osiris is no longer a direct participant in the drama, the story continues with struggles of his son Horus, destined to avenge Osiris and regain his throne. Horus was born secretly in the Delta marshes, hidden and protected by Isis. Various dangers such as snakes and scorpions threatened him, but with the magic of the gods to watch over him he grew to manhood and then set out to do battle with his uncle Seth and regain the throne.

The conflicts of Horus and Seth formed an epic struggle with a great many episodes, during the course of which neither god escaped injury, but Horus achieved the final victory of good over evil.

The myth of Osiris contains two main themes, one political and the other agricultural. In political terms, the myth preserves some dim historical elements of the time before Egypt's unification and the struggles between Upper Egypt and Delta chieftains. The myth also serves to strengthen the passage of kingship from father to son, not brother to brother.

In agricultural terms, Osiris's death and resurrection make him an early nature god, celebrated each year in simple ceremonies at the time of the Nile flood, when the seed crop was sown and when the harvest was gathered. In ritual terms the old agricultural ceremonies were joined with the cult of the dead to form the official Osirian rites and festivals. These were mainly performed at the places where parts of the body of Osiris were reputed to have been found or buried, such as Dendera, Abydos and Memphis.

period of Egyptian history, his titles indicate that the office he held was divine. He was the leader of both religious and secular life in Egypt, and he was an absolute monarch who ruled for the duration of his life.

In principle the king led all activities; in reality a complex hierarchy of bureaucrats, numbering in the thousands, was appointed to serve as advisors and functionaries in carrying out the details of running the country. During the Early Dynastic, as in the later Old Kingdom, many of the high officials were members of the royal family. Theoretically any

---

BOX 9.3 ◆ **Kings' names**

In the Early Dynastic the king at his coronation took three names (five names in later periods), each representing a facet of his dual kingship: the Horus, *nebty* and *nesu-bit* names.

The Horus name was written inside a rectangular box called a *serekh*, which represented the king's palace with its recessed panelling called niching. Surmounting the *serekh* was the falcon Horus, who was identified with the sun god, the living king and avenger of Osiris. The Horus name took precedence over all other names, and it is the name by which we know and refer to the early kings of Egypt.

The *nebti* name refers to 'the Two Ladies' of the land, represented by the vulture goddess Nekhbet of Upper Egypt and the Cobra goddess Wadjet of Lower Egypt. The title above the king's second name signifies that he is ruler of both Upper and Lower Egypt. The *nebti* name goes back at least to the time of King Aha, at the beginning of Dynasty 1.

The *nesu-bit* name, literally 'he of the reed and bee', refers, once again, to the king as ruler of Upper and Lower Egypt, but the exact meaning and relationship of the reed and sedge as a symbol of Upper Egypt and the bee of Lower Egypt remain a mystery. The *nesu-bit* name first appears in the reign of King Den of Dynasty 1 but may have existed earlier.

---

qualified person could enter the civil service, including women, but in practice it was composed predominantly of upper-class males.

At the head of this burgeoning civil service was the *chaty*, commonly translated as 'vizier'. The position of *chaty* dates to at least the beginning of Dynasty 3, but probably existed in some form as early as Narmer's reign. The *chaty*'s titles suggest he was something of a prime minister. Next to the king, the vizier was the highest legal authority of the land. Thus he was the highest court official and also served as the king's closest advisor. A position attributed to the *chaty* in one of his titles, 'he of the curtain' expresses his role perfectly: he was always present, even if not seen.

> **BOX 9.4 ◆ Viziers**
>
> The title 'vizier' is based on the Arabic word *wazir*. The closest approx-
> imation to the ancient Egyptian administrative position, *chaty*, is that
> of the Ottoman *vizier* and hence the adoption of the latter term as a
> label for this administrative position.

In the formative period of Egyptian government, Dynasties 1–3, many
departments were formed to aid the king in governing the land. Precisely
what these departments did and how (or if) they evolved into the known
units of the later historic period remains unclear. One office that certainly
existed by Dynasty 1 was that which dealt with the collection of taxes.

Inscriptions from the tomb of Ka, Narmer and Aha suggest that taxes
were collected in two divisions: Upper Egypt and Lower Egypt. This
not only reinforces the Egyptians' own mental division of the land into
two separate entities, but it also underlines the differences between the
types of produce that might come from these areas. A subdivision of the
treasury, called the *per-shena*, may have been responsible for storing
agricultural produce brought to the state through taxes and foundations.
By the end of Dynasty 2 we see the *per-hery-wedjeb*, an institution closely
connected with the *per-shena* and thought to be the 'house of redistribution', which as the name implies would pay out the stored goods to state
employees and provincial cults throughout the land.

At the local level the Egyptian government was composed of a series
of administrative districts called *sepat*, now more commonly referred to
by the Greek word *nome* (Fig. 9.1). The earliest documented evidence for
the existence of the *sepat* is Dynasty 3, during the reign of Djoser, but
they very likely existed in some form earlier. Essentially a *sepat* was a
miniature version of the state: the chief or governor of the district ruled
it like a miniature kingdom but without the obvious opulence afforded to
the king. *Sepats* were not, as was once thought, vestiges of earlier prehistoric chiefdoms, but rather seem to be administrative creations of the
ruling elite.

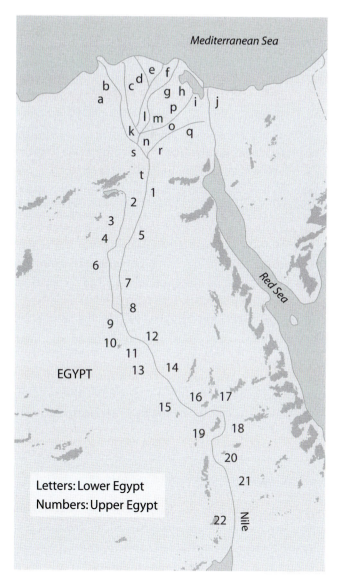

FIGURE 9.1 ◆ *Approximate location of the Egyptian nomes as defined in later*
periods.   Source: After Baines, John and Malek, Jaromir, *Atlas of Ancient Egypt*
                    (Phaidon, 1980), courtesy of Lovell Johns. Redrawn by Brenda Coelho

By the Early Dynastic Period the state received its funding through one of two sources: (a) royal foundations, where agricultural lands and other holdings were worked for the sole purpose of providing personal income to the king, paying court officials and covering other expenses related to his office, and (b) taxation of the general populace, which financed the government payroll as well as provided a surplus for times of need. Taxes could be paid in tangible goods or physical (*corvée*) labour. The *corvée* labour (labour drafted from the ranks of the peasantry) was directed towards state and community projects such as working on the royal tomb or clearing irrigation canals. Naturally the state provided for all needs while inducted.

Trade was an integral part of the economy, so it seems ironic that no currency, coinage or distinct merchant class existed. Bartering for goods was the basic means of exchange, and upper-middle-class bureaucrats filled the role of merchants. These people, generally royal officials or members of strong ruling families that led the local *sepat* governments, held sway over local trade networks. The king held a monopoly on international trade, and through taxation of all trade, local and international, his office held the wealth of the nation.

Although there are implications of scuffles with desert peoples, Libyans and other enemies of Egypt, we have no evidence to support the existence of a standing army during the Early Dynastic Period. Given the

---

BOX 9.5 ◆ Weapons

Military weapons carried by the Egyptian soldier were minimal: no body armour was used, nor were shields prevalent. Based on depictions of battle scenes, weapons consisted of bow and arrow, mace, battle-axe or club, boomerang, daggers and thrusting spears. No wooden bows of the period are known, but numerous arrows have been found: blunt-head arrows, arrows tipped with barbed catfish spines, smooth pointed arrows and arrows with metal points. The battle mace was pear-shaped or elliptical, the former often seen in scenes where the king is smiting a subdued enemy. Spears could have copper or stone tips and daggers were made of copper or flint.

proximity in time to Egypt's unification, at least some aspects of which involved armed conflict, it is hard to believe that some military presence did not exist. It may be that a core of officers maintained a presence but regular troops were conscripted from the countryside for temporary duty. Conscripts were probably called to service based on a quota system for each *sepat*, and they carried out their service within that group, being led by a local ruler from their province.

Little can be said with certainty about the priesthood at this time. Later, individuals who devoted all their time to the cult headed the priesthood of large temples, but the ranks were filled with part-timers who held secular positions and may even have served as priests for different cults at different temples or shrines. How this system evolved and whether it existed at the dawn of the Dynastic Period is not known. Nevertheless, even given the paucity of textual data for the Early Dynastic, we do know that many of the gods well-known in later periods were worshipped at or near the time of unification. Most of the gods of this period were presented in animal form, but by the middle of Dynasty 2 they took on anthropomorphic shapes, usually with a human body and an animal head. Already by the Early Dynastic Period, we see Horus as a symbol of kingship and avenger of Osiris. Seth, Horus's arch-enemy, also must have been part of the pantheon from early on, since Khasekhemui took Seth's name as part of his royal insignia at the end of Dynasty 2. The sun god Re seems to have been worshipped by the early dynasties, as were Anubis (Wepwawet – guardian of the cemetery), Hathor (the benevolent cow goddess) and Apis (bull-god of Memphis), as well as others not so well known to the general public such as Min (god of the traveller and fertility), Ptah (a creator deity), Seshet (goddess of learning) and Mehit (lion goddess) (See Fig. 9.2.).

The role of the scribe and the general literacy of the population during the first three dynasties remain a mystery. Clearly, few people knew how to read and write: throughout most of the Dynastic Period only about 1 per cent of the population was literate. This figure was probably even lower for the Early Dynastic Period for the simple reason that the need for record-keeping had yet to reach its full potential and therefore the bureaucracy had not yet reached the complexity of later periods. Given the many years of training necessary to be a scribe, the scribe's position, whether formalised at this time or not, was one of importance.

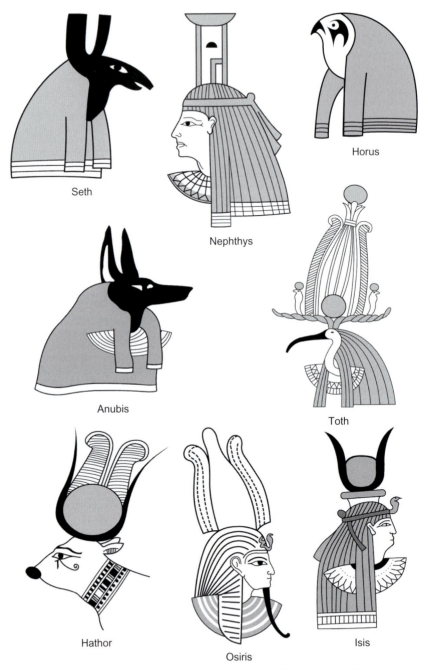

Seth

Nephthys

Horus

Anubis

Toth

Hathor

Osiris

Isis

FIGURE 9.2 ◆ *Late Period renditions of popular gods of the Early Dynastic.*

Source: Redrawn by Carolynn Govoni

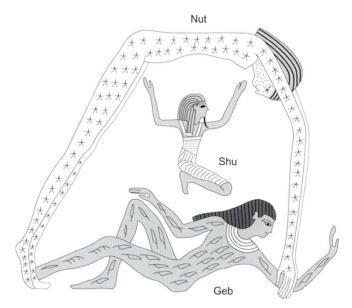

Nut

Shu

Geb

FIGURE 9.2 ◆ (*continued*)

The craftsmen and the peasantry

Skilled labourers and artisans filled out the lower rungs of the middle class, and the herdsmen and farm peasantry, who were responsible for Egypt's tremendous agricultural productivity and surplus wealth, occupied the lowest station on the social ladder. The Early Dynastic craftsmen and craftswomen were highly specialised and, as in Old Kingdom times, probably inherited their trade from their parents or other family members, their skills undoubtedly learned through apprenticeship. It is unclear if the practitioners of some crafts or trades were considered of higher status than others. As in later periods, men usually filled these roles, but certain trades probably had skilled women practitioners, particularly textiles and pottery manufacturers. Many craftsmen worked as part of a temple or estate or, as in medieval Europe, through a local guild. Furniture, statues, textiles, perfumes and pottery were all products of the craftsmen class. Probably the most common of the craft professions was the potter. Every town and village had its own potter, and even under the strong government of Dynasties 4 and 5, when national styles

---

BOX 9.6 ◆ Ceramic bowl analysis

Statistical (measured metric) analyses of ceramic bowls found at
Dynasty 4 Giza, Kom el-Hisn and Mendes clearly show each possessed
local stylistic traits, and, although they might not appear different to
the untrained eye, archaeologists can distinguish them.

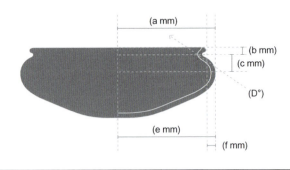

---

dominated the shape and forms of pottery, provincial traits can still be
identified.

In ancient times the ability to produce agricultural surpluses meant
economic power, which meant that by Dynasty 1 Egypt was the world's
first superpower. From Predynastic times on and throughout Egyptian
history, the vast majority of the population was engaged in farming, with
grain as the main agricultural product (see Figs 9.3 and 9.4).

The average Egyptian farmer, called *mrjw* ('those of the canal'), was
basically a field hand who worked the land for others in exchange for part
of the harvest. The farm itself was not usually a contiguous piece of land
but through heredity and purchases was composed of many plots scattered over a region. If not working the farm himself, the landowner leased
the land to a cultivator who worked the land or hired farm hands to carry
out the labour. How a crop was divided between cultivator, landowner
and field hands is not clear even for the better documented periods, but
estimates from the later dynasties suggest the harvest was split evenly
between owner and cultivator. The farm labourers also received some
portion of the harvest, but exactly how much is not known. In some
instances the labourers' wages were augmented by a gratuity: they were

FIGURE 9.3 ◆ *Wheat and barley, the major crops of Ancient Egypt, were grown in great abundance and provided legendary surpluses of food.*

Source: Photograph by D. J. Brewer

FIGURE 9.4 ◆ *Granaries, like this New Kingdom example, held Egypt's agricultural wealth. Grain had to be collected, stored and redistributed from these containers, so a large bureaucracy was needed to maintain records.*

Source: Photograph by D. J. Brewer

allowed to keep all the produce they could glean in one day from the harvested fields. The farmer's counterpart in the livestock trade, the herder, similarly exploited his skill for sustenance, often spending long periods of time away from his ancestral home herding and caring for cattle, sheep and goats belonging to someone else. Considered among the lowest members of the peasant class were fishermen. Why such an aversion to fisher folk? It may be simply that fish and those who caught, prepared and sold them smelled – as one text noted, 'Behold my name (reputation) stinks, more than a catch of fish on a hot day'. The ancient Egyptian word for 'bad smells' included a hieroglyph of a fish in the spelling, and a depiction of a fish was also used in writing the word for 'forbidden' or 'taboo'.

Although Egypt professed to be an upwardly mobile society, in reality those who were born to a particular class probably lived out their lives in that class, as did their descendants. There was, however, always the chance that they might be noticed by a member of the elite or royal family and hired into their estate or even the household. Craftsmen of exceptional skill probably had the best chance of achieving such a distinction, but skilled herdsmen and farm managers too could utilise their talents for the prestige of working on a nobleman's estate, in a temple or even at the palace. Nothing, however, could put you on the fast track to success better than learning to read and write, but such opportunities were rare outside the families of scribes who passed on their learned trade to their descendants.

Family life

The nuclear family – husband, wife and children – was the core of Egyptian society throughout its history. People took pride in their family, and lineage was traced through both the mother's and the father's lines. Respect for one's parents was a cornerstone of morality, and the most fundamental duty of the eldest son was to care for his parents in their last days and to ensure that they received a proper burial.

Although countless genealogical lists demonstrate how important family ties were, Egyptian kinship terms, ironically, lacked specific words to identify blood relatives beyond the immediate family. For example, the word used to designate 'mother' was also used for 'grandmother', and the word for 'father' was the same as 'grandfather'; similarly, the terms for 'son', 'grandson' and 'nephew' (or 'daughter', 'granddaughter' and 'niece') were identical. 'Uncle' and 'brother' (or 'aunt' and 'sister') were also designated by the same word. To make matters even more confusing, the term 'sister' was often used for 'wife', perhaps an indication of the strength of the bond between spouses.

The king, as holder of a divine office, could have many wives; however, one wife, usually his first, was the queen and the first son she bore would be next in line to rule Egypt. It is not known if the custom of brother–sister marriages, which ensured the next generation would have as much divinity as possible, was practised at this time. On those occasions when the royal couple did not produce a male heir, the son of a lesser wife could be named king-apparent. Barring this, a more distant male relative could ascend to the throne, but palace intrigue usually resulted.

Mortal Egyptians (as opposed to divine kings) were monogamous. As in later times, affection was most likely expressed by rubbing noses (a symbolic exchange of breath, or life) or by kissing. Egyptians were highly sensual people, and a major theme of their religion was fertility and procreation.

Although most of our information on marriage comes from later texts, the basic principles probably existed in the Early Dynastic Period. The ancient Egyptian terms for marriage, *meni* ('to moor [a boat]') and *grg pr* ('to found a house'), convey the sense that the arrangement was like that of our own culture – a new beginning for the couple. Later documents indicate that the groom often gave the bride's family a gift and also gave his betrothed presents. Legal texts of later dynasties indicate that each spouse maintained control of the property that they brought to the marriage, while property acquired during the union was jointly held. Ideally the new couple lived in their own house, but if that was impossible they lived with one of their parents. Considering the lack of effective contraceptives, most women probably became pregnant shortly after marriage.

Men and women inherited equally (and often separately) from their parents, a practice that probably dates back to the Predynastic Period. The eldest son often, but not always, inherited his father's job and position (whether in a workshop or temple), but to him also fell the onerous and costly responsibility of his parents' proper burial. Real estate generally was not divided among heirs but was held jointly by the family members.

A family member could leave property to a person other than the expected heirs, but it is not known if the use of a formal document called an *imeyt-per* ('that which is in the house') existed at this early time. The *imeyt-per* was like a living will and would ensure that the wishes of the deceased were carried out.

In Egyptian households of all classes, children of both sexes were valued and wanted. The birth of a child was, therefore, a time of great joy, but also one of serious concern, given the high rate of infant mortality and the stress of childbirth on the mother.

Data collected from modern non-industrial societies suggest that one of the best ways to maintain a healthy infant under the less than sanitary conditions that prevailed in ancient times was by breast-feeding. In addition to the transfer of antibodies through mother's milk, breast-feeding also offered the infant some protection from food-borne diseases and contaminated water. Gastrointestinal disorders are common under poor sanitary conditions, and because infant immunity is reduced during weaning, childrens' susceptibility to disease increases at this time. Indirect evidence for this in ancient Egypt comes from a number of cemeteries where the childhood death rate peaks at about age four, which correlates with an Egyptian child's introduction to solid foods (Egyptian women are thought to have breast-fed their children for about three years). Prolonged lactation offered a number of heath advantages to the mother as well – primarily, through hormonally suppressing ovulation, it reduced the chance of conceiving another child too soon, which allowed the mother more time between pregnancies.

Egyptian children who lived through their fifth year could generally look forward to a full life, which in Early Dynastic times was about 33 years for men and 29 years for women, based on skeletal evidence. Upper-class males, who were generally better fed and performed less strenuous labour than the lower classes, could expect a much longer life extending into the fifties, sixties and even seventies. Upper-class women also looked forward to a longer life than women from the lower classes, but the arduous task of bearing many children resulted in a lower life expectancy for women in general, compared with their male counterparts.

The end of childhood appears to have been marked by the onset of menses for girls and the ceremony of circumcision for boys. That circumcision was a ritual transition from boyhood to manhood is indicated by

Dynastic Period references such as 'When I was a boy, before my foreskin was removed from me'. The extent to which male circumcision was practised is not known: mummies of later dynasties show that some males were circumcised while others were not. Recent research on the age of puberty suggests that males probably reached sexual maturity at 14 and females around 12 or 13 years of age.

The home

Compared with funerary architecture, very little is known of ancient Egyptian domestic architecture of any period. One of the main problems in acquiring information about houses is that they were made of perishable materials; additionally, until recent years there was little interest in excavating domestic – as opposed to funerary or monumental – architecture, because it produces little in the way of museum-quality artefacts.

The recovery of miniature houses made of clay, dating to Late Naqada III and the Early Dynastic Period, suggests that the most common home was a simple rectangular mud brick structure with a flat roof. These models, like those in the later periods, are thought to represent homes for the soul, and their appearance, like other artistic renditions of the tomb, is thought to mimic actual houses (Fig. 9.5). These small rectangular homes might seem confining to us but are appropriately substantial within the context of Egyptian culture and economics. Unlike Euro-American culture, the Egyptian concept of living quarters extended beyond the walls of the home. In ancient Egypt, as in many modern peasant villages, many activities were carried out in front of the home, on the roof or in the streets. The Early Dynastic Egyptians' concept of private and public space differed from that of our own, a difference reflected in the space requirements deemed essential for a house.

Perhaps as early as Dynasty 1, but certainly by the end of Dynasty 3, houses of wealthier Egyptians were multi-roomed (Fig. 9.5b). The main entrance of such houses led to a reception room; private quarters were located in the back, shielded from prying eyes and ears. If the house was located in a crowded community, storage containers for grain and other needs were located on top of the home or within a courtyard. In rural areas storage facilities were often located beside the home. Based on excavations, this general house plan was still in use by many classes

FIGURE 9.5 ◆ *A soul house was created for the afterlife, but, like other aspects of burial, probably resembles a contemporary dwelling of the deceased: (a) represents a typical village dwelling and (b) a larger, more complex soul house for a member of the upper class.*

Sources: (a) © Copyright The British Museum; (b) Copyright Petrie Museum of Egyptian Archaeology, University College London

of society in the New Kingdom, over 1,000 years later. Naturally, the size and number of rooms increased with the fortune of the owner, and larger homes might even have a second floor, balcony, staircase or other amenities.

Dress and fashion

The most common fabric for Early Dynastic clothing for both genders was linen. Because linen is very hard to dye, most clothes were off-white, so colour was added through belts, sashes and other adornments such as jewellery.

Women's standard apparel from the earliest dynasties into the New Kingdom was the sheath dress (Fig. 9.6). Interestingly, the skin-tight

FIGURE 9.6 ◆ *Tomb scene depicting a common dress worn by women from the Early Dynastic through to the later periods. The form-fitting style is very likely 'an ideal' rather than a reflection of its actual fit.*

Source: Photograph by D. J. Brewer

dress so often depicted in tomb scenes would have been impractical for carrying out even modest physical tasks, suggesting the representations are idealised.

The typical garment worn by men was a kilt, made of a rectangular piece of linen cloth wrapped rather loosely around the hips, leaving the knees uncovered (Plate 25). This garment was the standard male attire for all classes from peasants to royalty, though the quality of the linen and the style varied according to one's purchasing power. Though styles changed over time, the simple kilt remained the standard garb for scribes, servants and peasants.

Apparently, regardless of the season, occasion or social class, Egyptians preferred to go barefoot. During the Early Dynastic Period, women never wore shoes or sandals. Men, if they wore shoes at all, wore them only outside. Even then they often removed them, giving them to a sandal-bearer, who would follow his employer, wash his feet and provide the sandals at the appropriate time. A scene from the Narmer Palette presents an excellent example of this practice (Fig. 9.7).

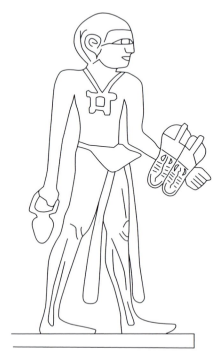

FIGURE 9.7 ◆ *The sandal-bearer of King Narmer.*

Source: Redrawn by Brenda Coelho

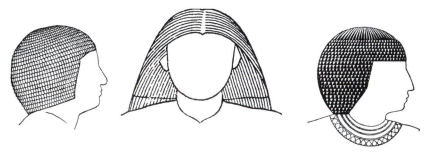

FIGURE 9.8 ◆ *Common male hairstyles of the Early Dynastic and Old Kingdom.*   *Source*: Redrawn by Brenda Coelho

FIGURE 9.9 ◆ *A noble holding a staff, which carried with it a message of authority. It remains unclear if different types of staffs reflect different ranks or affiliations.*

Source: Photograph by D. J. Brewer

In the early dynasties, women wore their hair (or wigs) long and straight. From the limited pictorial evidence, it is not known if men wore wigs, but it does seem likely (Fig. 9.8). Fashion statements were made with accessories such as jewellery and ribbons. Men also carried staffs that marked status and social class (Fig. 9.9). Both genders wore copious

FIGURE 9.10 ◆ *Simple make-up vessel and applicators.*

Source: Courtesy of the Spurlock Museum, University of Illinois

amounts of perfumes and cosmetics made of ground minerals and earth pigments. Eye shadows were green, made of crushed malachite, and dark grey, made from galena. Red powder made from haematite was also used, perhaps to enhance cheek colour. Delicate ivory and wood sticks were used to apply the make-up, while small vessels of alabaster, marble and crystal held unguents and other fragrant materials (Fig. 9.10).

Entertainment

There is much evidence for the leisure activities of the ancient Egyptians, many of which had their roots in the Pre- and Early Dynastic Period. Men engaged in physical sports, such as hunting, fishing and archery, and both men and women enjoyed swimming. We know board games were played, because examples have been recovered from a number of localities. Moves on board games were determined by throw sticks, which, like dice, made a game of chance out of the next move (Fig. 9.11).

Tomb paintings suggest that banquets were a popular form of relaxation throughout the Dynastic Period, at least for the upper class. At such

FIGURE 9.11 ◆ *An Early Dynastic gaming board.*

Source: Courtesy of the Egypt Exploration Society

FIGURE 9.12 ◆ *A New Kingdom banquet, clearly demonstrating that the partygoers were separated by gender.*

Source: Erich Lessing/Art Resource, NY. Tomb of Nakht, Thebes, Egypt

events food, alcoholic beverages, music and dancing were common. Although the organisation of the tomb scenes may be misleading, it seems that proprieties of the times kept male and female guests seated apart (Fig. 9.12).

The foundation of all daily or banquet meals, regardless of social class, was the same: bread, beer and produce. The last included leeks, onions, garlic, beans, peas, lentils and several varieties of melons. Wealthy Egyptians enjoyed red meat, honey-sweetened cakes and other delicacies. Lower-class Egyptians relied on fish and fowl for most of their meat proteins and only rarely enjoyed honey-sweetened treats. The ready availability of Nile fish and fowl made them inexpensive, while beef and to a varying extent other red meats were costly and considered a luxury.

The national drink in ancient Egypt was beer, and all ancient Egyptians – rich and poor, male and female – drank great quantities of it. Wages were paid in grain, which was used to make the two staples of the Egyptian diet, bread and beer. Beer was made from barley dough, so bread-making and beer-making are often shown together in artistic

---

BOX 9.7 ◆ **Egyptian meal**

We know something of the foods of the period thanks to the tradition of leaving the deceased a funerary meal, some of which have been recovered fully intact. One such example is the final meal of a Saqqara Dynasty 2 lady of lesser nobility, which included:

- a form of porridge or gruel made from ground barley
- a cooked quail, cleaned and dressed with the head tucked under the wing
- two cooked kidneys
- a pigeon stew
- a cooked fish, cleaned and dressed with head removed
- beef ribs
- small triangular loaves of bread
- small round cakes
- stewed fruit, possibly figs
- fresh Nabk berries (not unlike a cherry)

With the meal were small jars thought to contain some form of cheese and large pottery vessels for wine and beer. Admittedly this was a sumptuous feast beyond the means of most of Egypt's populace, but it does provide a good indication of the foods available. From pictures on Dynasty 2 stelae we know that geese were also eaten. Vegetables were also abundant beyond belief, including lettuce, leeks, onions, garlic and many types of melons. Salt was available for seasoning, as was honey for sweetening.

---

composition. Excavations at Hierakonpolis, where beer- and bread-making areas were juxtaposed, support the artistic relationship (Fig. 9.13).

To make beer, barley was partially baked and then crumbled into a large vat, where it was mixed with water and sometimes sweetened with date juice. This mixture was left to ferment, which it did quickly; the liquid was then strained into a pot that was sealed with a clay stopper (Fig. 9.14). Because it went flat very quickly, ancient Egyptian beer had to be drunk soon after it was made. Egyptians made a variety of beers of

(a)

(b)

FIGURE 9.13 ◆ *Breweries and bakeries (a) at Hierakonpolis were built close to each other, probably because the ingredients were similar. Residues of beer ingredients still remain in the vats (b).*

Source: © Jeremy Geller

(c)

FIGURE 9.13 ◆ *(continued) (c) Residues of beer ingredients recovered from vats after more than 5,000 years.*

different strengths; alcoholic strength was based on how much beer was made from one *hekat* (4.54 litres) of barley – the fewer measures of beer made per unit of barley, the stronger the brew.

In addition to beer, wine was also drunk. Jar labels with notations that the wine was from the 'Vineyard of King Djet' indicate that wine production was well established as early as Dynasty 1. It is difficult to speculate how Egyptian wine tasted. Nevertheless, because of the climate, low acid (sweet) grapes probably predominated, which would have resulted in a sweet, rather than dry, wine. Alcohol content would have varied considerably from area to area and from vintage to vintage, but generally Egyptian wine probably had a lower alcohol content than modern table wines.

As in any modern celebration, along with eating and drinking went dance and song. Dancing seems to have been a spectator sport in which professionals performed for the guests. Females and males are never depicted dancing together as pairs; males danced with males and females

FIGURE 9.14 ◆ *Beer-making scene from a Dynasty 5 tomb, which demonstrates the process of creating the ancient brew.*

Source: After Brewer, Redford and Redford, *Domestic Plants and Animals: The Egyptian Origins* (Aris and Phillips, 1994). Courtesy of Oxbow Books. Redrawn by Brenda Coelho

with females. Singers, accompanied by musical instruments, entertained guests at private parties, public functions or even in the palace.

Ancient Egyptians played a variety of musical instruments. Of the wind instruments, one of the oldest was the reed or wood flute. The flute always remained popular among Egyptians and it has survived to this day as the Arabic *nay* and *uffafa*. Also popular during the Early Dynastic were various percussion instruments, ranging from bone or ivory clappers to hand-rattles and drums. Drums of all sizes were played using fingers and hands; sticks were not used.

A less formal type of entertainment could be found at inns and beer houses, where the strict proprieties of higher society did not extend. In

BOX 9.8 ◆ Beer recipe

Modern versions of ancient beer called *bouza* remain a part of rural Egyptian life. *Bouza* is made in a very similar manner to that of the ancient brew. First, wheat or barley is coarsely grated and placed in a basin and kneaded with water into a dough. The dough is cut into thick loaves and lightly baked. Additional grain that has been left to germinate and then dried in the sun is added to the baked dough and mixed with water. This concoction is then left to ferment for 24 hours at air temperature. The fermented mixture is then sieved to remove solid materials and the alcoholic liquid is ready for consumption either as is or in a diluted form.

the pubs of the day, drinking often led to singing, dancing and gaming, and males and females were free to interact with each other. Taverns stayed open late into the night, and patrons drank beer in such quantities that intoxication was not uncommon.

The streets of the larger Early Dynastic towns no doubt had a number of 'beer halls', and later texts refer to the 'harlots' who could be found there. Proverbs warning young men to avoid fraternisation with 'a woman who has no house' indicate that some form of prostitution existed in ancient Egyptian society, probably from the onset of the Naqada III Period, when large population centres emerged.

BOX 9.9 ◆ Wary of harlots

'He who makes love to a woman of the street will have his purse cut open on its side.'

In summary, life during the Predynastic, Early Dynastic and Later Dynastic Periods had many similarities: it centred on family, and one's profession was often tied to heredity. Although the workday was arduous, particularly for those labouring in the fields, numerous entertainment outlets existed, from eloquent parties to rowdy beer halls and the businesses that such endeavours attracted.

CHAPTER 10

. . . .

New horizons

Our most impressive archaeological evidence for Egypt's transformation from its prehistoric antecedents to its new role as the world's first great civilisation is the pyramids. Only a stable, well-organised government could divert such a huge labour force and finances to produce these massive and enduring monuments, and it is in pyramid building that all aspects of Egyptian culture intersect: agriculture, craft production, trade, religion and centralised government. This achievement marks the end of Egypt's Early Dynastic Period and ushers in the beginning of the classic period of Egyptian history – the Old Kingdom, or pyramid age.

It is difficult to characterise any complex culture using only a few words, yet popular clichés derived from recognisable traits are often employed as descriptive markers. When one thinks of France, for example, fine wine and food come to mind, while Italy is known for its fashion, Britain for its people's strong character and America for its ingenuity. When one thinks of ancient Egypt, what usually comes to mind are the preparations that were made for the end of life. No culture could send you to the next world in greater style than the Egyptian. While the attention and resources lavished upon death seem unimaginable from our modern perspective and might lead some to believe that Egyptians looked forward to death, on the contrary, Egyptians loved life, and, as in our culture, death was an uncomfortable concept.

'If you think of burial, it is agony;
it is the bringing of tears through making a man miserable;
it is taking a man from his house,
being cast upon the high ground,
You shall not come up again to see suns . . .'

[*Dialogue of a Man with his Soul*, Parkinson 1991]

The Egyptians' solution to this frightening prospect was to transform death into something less fearful – death became a simple transition from the life they knew on Earth to an eternal existence in an afterworld similar to what they had experienced in life.

To ensure life in the hereafter, several requirements had to be met. First, the body had to be preserved as a home or anchor for the soul. Thus the practice of preserving the physical remains of the deceased became important. Second, the body also had to be recognisable, so that the part of the soul that travelled beyond the tomb would know where to return each night.

BOX 10.1 ◆ Preparation of the dead for eternal life

Egyptian belief in an afterlife evolved some time in the Paleolithic and by Predynastic times was already a well-established custom. Cemeteries were situated away from villages, usually on the Nile's left bank, the west being associated with the setting sun and the land of the departed. The bodies of deceased peasants were buried much as they had been for generations before, but graves for the wealthier classes began to take on more and more grave goods. Because of the custom of interring bodies with precious goods, grave-robbing accompanied the development of Egyptian burial practices. After such burials had been pillaged, the bodies were sometimes exposed and the Egyptians noticed that they had been desiccated by the hot desert sands and naturally preserved. Perhaps from this evolved the belief that the body had to be preserved for the soul to live eternally in the hereafter.

As society began to diversify in the Late Predynastic, the wealthy preferred to be buried in larger and more elaborate tombs. Because their bodies were now placed in a coffin or chamber and surrounded by air rather than hot desiccating sands, they decomposed. It seems that by the First Dynasty the Egyptians sought to achieve by artificial means some semblance of the preservation of the body that had been achieved naturally

---

in sand graves. The method of encircling the torso, limbs and digits with layers of fine linen became standard practice in the Early Dynastic. The linen was impregnated with resin, and often physical features were moulded on the body to give it some semblance of gender. (The practice of removing the internal organs did not occur until Dynasty 4.) The bodies were still flexed as in Predynastic times, placed in a basket or ceramic sarcophagus and interred. This did not save the body from decomposing, because modern excavations show the linen in direct contact with the skeleton, but it apparently satisfied the basic needs for a life after death.

BOX 10.2 ◆ The Egyptian soul

The Egyptians believed that the soul was composed of different aspects. One part was the *ka*, an individual's life-energy, perceived as a person's physical double. It was depicted in the same form as the living person, in some cases with the hieroglyph for *ka* (two upraised hands) over the head of the figure. Although the *ka* was believed to be created at birth and present throughout the person's lifetime, most discussions of the *ka* were in reference to life after death; indeed the phrase 'to go to one's *ka*' was a euphemism for 'to die'. The *ka* had material needs such as food and drink even after death, and it is to the *ka* that such offerings were made. The *ba*, another division of the soul, represented your individuality or personality and was portrayed as a bird with a human head. It was able to maintain communication between the land of the living and the afterlife. The *ba* was believed to stay with the deceased in the tomb during the night, but during the day it left to spend time in the sunshine. The *ba* could not function if the corpse was decaying, so preserving the body was necessary to ensure the *ba*'s survival.

The third aspect, the *akh*, was the transfigured blessed spirit that survived death. It was a luminous element that conferred *akh*-hood after death; it was the power, the spirit of the deceased. The *akh* was represented as the person (him or herself) and was thought in its transfigured form to mingle with the gods. It could also reach across the divide and influence the world of the living in a positive or negative manner. Thus it had some parallel to our concept of 'ghost'.

Third, because the soul had to be sustained with food, beverages and the things that individuals had used and enjoyed during their lifetime, a tomb – referred to as 'a house of eternity' – had to be built and serve as a warehouse, stocked with everything the deceased required in the next life. So important were the concepts of life after death and of sustaining that life that, by the end of the Early Dynastic Period, multiple levels of 'heaven insurance' were built into the tomb. Long after death, offerings of food and other tangible needs of the deceased were supposed to be brought to the tomb by family members, cult priests or other worshippers on a regular basis in order to sustain the soul, but, should these gifts not be forthcoming, the pictures of offerings painted or carved in relief on the tomb walls could substitute for the real thing (see Fig. 9.6). The Egyptians believed that even a written reference could substitute for the actual object, so the walls of tombs were not only decorated with scenes of offerings, but also with standardised texts listing food and drink (Fig. 10.1)

FIGURE 10.1 ◆ *An Old Kingdom false door with the standard text offering of 'bread and beer' to the deceased for eternity. Simply reciting the text in honour of the tomb owner will ensure sustenance in the hereafter.*

Source: Photograph by D. J. Brewer

designed to provide for the deceased's needs if the other levels of insurance failed. Tomb walls were also decorated with scenes of family life and the activities that the deceased enjoyed in life and hoped to enjoy in the afterlife.

The earliest private (non-royal) tombs were oval pits, sometimes lined with mats. The body was placed in a contracted position, accompanied by a few pots of beer and food and perhaps a palette upon which to grind cosmetics (see Fig. 6.18). No superstructures have survived from these earliest tombs, but it is assumed that the pit was covered with a mound of earth that symbolised the mound of creation from which all life sprang, thereby ensuring the individual's rebirth.

By the first two dynasties, this simple mound had evolved into a rectangular structure called a *mastaba* (from the Arabic for 'bench') (Fig. 10.2). *Mastabas* could range from several square metres to over 5,000 square metres.

The *mastaba* can be divided into three major sections: the excavated substructure, the mud brick superstructure and the ancillary structures. The substructure consisted of a pit cut into the earth or rock. In more elaborate tombs this area was subdivided into a burial chamber and four adjacent storage rooms, which were used to hold the most valuable of the funerary goods. Because the burial chamber was the most important of the rooms, it was often decorated. One excavated Early Dynastic tomb contained wooden pilasters decorated with inlaid gold and another was decorated with coloured woven mats. The burial chamber held the coffined body of the deceased, a funerary meal, a chest of clothing and furniture. The adjacent storerooms held jewellery, games, more furniture, tools, weapons and additional foods. Atop the burial chamber, after the deceased was interred, a mound of earth was constructed. Although its shape is unknown because no intact mound has been discovered, it might have been simply a pile of earth or perhaps a sculpted pyramidal mound. The tomb's above-ground structure served (Fig. 10.2) as a second floor composed of additional storage chambers. The structure was situated over the burial chamber, its mound and any adjacent storage or offering rooms. It was essentially a mud-brick rectangle, divided into a series of storerooms for less valuable funerary equipment. In the larger tombs, each room held articles of similar type, such as weapons and games, furniture and food and drink. The interior walls were probably decorated

(a)

(b)

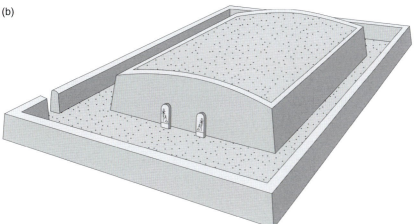

FIGURE 10.2 ◆ *(a) The Old Kingdom* mastaba *complex surrounding the Giza* pyramids; *(b) an artist's conception of a Delta* mastaba.

Sources: (a) Photograph by D. J. Brewer;
(b) After Spencer, A. J., *The Rise of Civilisation in the Nile Valley*,
courtesy of the Trustees of the British Museum. Redrawn by Brenda Coelho

FIGURE 10.2 ◆ *(continued) The excavation of a Delta mastaba (c) from the above ground structure; (d) through the storage chambers.*

Source: Courtesy of Bernard Bothmer

FIGURE 10.2 ◆ *(continued) (e) into the burial chamber.*

in some manner, but because they were made of mud brick and plaster little has survived. While Early Dynastic *mastaba* tombs at Saqqara have provided some insights into exterior tomb decorations of the period, whether these styles extended to Upper Egypt or to all tombs, as opposed to royal tombs, is not known.

At Saqqara remains of colourful geometric patterns were found on the tombs' niched exterior façade, as well as on some of the corridors within the *mastaba* (Plates 26 and 27). In general, the mud-brick walls had been faced with gypsum stucco on which were painted elaborate designs.

In theory, tombs of all types were to be located on the west bank of the Nile, the land of the setting sun and of the dead. In practice, tombs were located on either side of the river, but always on the desert edge, away from the valuable cultivable land.

Mastaba tomb architecture of the first kings did not differ significantly from the early *mastabas* of other powerful individuals. Like the early private *mastabas*, the first royal *mastabas* were composed of compart-mented subterranean chambers, presumably for the burial of the king and for the storage of grave goods, and a mud-brick superstructure. Beginning with the tomb of King Den (Dynasty 1), a stairway was incorporated in the tomb. This allowed access to the burial chamber after the tomb was completed and offered more time to outfit the tomb's interior with grave goods. Another interesting feature of Den's tomb was that the burial chamber was paved with blocks of Aswan granite – the same as the great pyramids.

The sides of royal *mastabas* were niched in imitation of the royal palace, emphasising the concept of the tomb as the eternal home of the deceased. Two stelae carved with the king's name stood to the east of the *mastaba*, presumably marking where funerary offerings were to be left. No royal *mastaba* roofs have been preserved, but we assume that they were slightly vaulted, in imitation of the mound of creation – much like the *gezira* mounds that sustained life amid the Nile's floodwaters. Even in this early period, it is clear that the royal tomb was only one part of a larger funerary complex: a niched wall surrounded the complex, and ritual boats, either real or stone imitations, were buried nearby to carry the king through his journey to the next world. Several *mastabas* at Saqqara had a low brick bench built around the entire base of the structure. Atop the bench were placed bulls' heads, fashioned out of clay, but with real cattle horns (Fig. 10.3). Other features of a royal complex included huge mud-brick enclosures, located away from the tomb near the river. These may have been massive mortuary temples with offering chapels. The best preserved of these is the massive 122 by 65 metre (400 by 213 ft) enclosure of Khasekhemui, formerly identified as a 'fort' (Fig. 10.4). One feature found only with First Dynasty royal tombs are subsidiary burials of courtiers, indicating that at this early date the king's retainers were sacrificed to accompany him into the afterlife so they could continue to serve his majesty (Fig. 10.5). For example, the tomb of Den was ringed by a series of mud-brick compartments that contained 338 subsidiary burials. These individuals were buried in such a way as to suggest they had been interred at the same time and died by ritual killing. After Dynasty I, because carved or painted representations could substitute for the actual thing, the tradition of sacrifice ceased to exist.

Changes in design of Dynasty I *mastabas* at Saqqara and Abydos offer, in embryonic form, elements of the later pyramids. For example, the sliding portcullis, the door that sealed the burial chamber, was incorporated into tombs at this time (Fig. 10.6). This allowed the burial chamber to be sealed while the rest of the tomb remained open for provisioning.

FIGURE 10.3 ◆ *A bull's horns bench uncovered at a Saqqara* mastaba *by early 20th-century archaeologists.* *Source*: Courtesy of the Egypt Exploration Society

FIGURE 10.4 ◆ *The 'Fort of Khasekhemui' located in the ancient city of Nekhen (Hierakonpolis).*   *Source:* © Jeremy Geller

Another feature of tombs of this period is an earthen mound placed over the burial chamber, which was symbolic of the mound of creation. Some *mastabas* contained chambers lined with coloured reed mats – forerunners to the faïence tiles found in chambers of the Step Pyramid at Saqqara (Plate 28).

FIGURE 10.5 ◆ *Some Early Dynastic royal tombs held as many as 300 graves belonging to the royal retainers. By their death and presence in burial they could continue to serve the king in the afterlife.*

Source: Courtesy of the Egypt Exploration Society

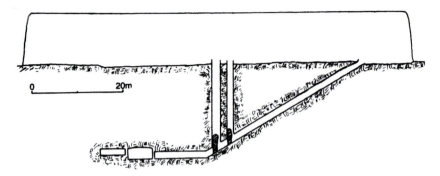

0   20m

FIGURE 10.6 ◆ *One of the earliest attempts to thwart tomb robbers was the sliding portcullis. Large stones slid into passageways to block entry. Like all later defences it did little to protect the deceased and his/her treasures.*

Source: Redrawn by Brenda Coelho and Loren Kirkwood

Perhaps the most vivid example foreshadowing the later pyramids was found at Saqqara. Here a 4 metre (13 ft) rectangular pit was surrounded by a mud brick wall rising 6 metre (20 ft) above the ground. Three sides of the wall were built outwards in a series of steps. This created a rectangular, albeit truncated, three-sided step pyramid (Fig. 10.7). Why the fourth side of the tomb wall was not stepped remains a mystery. Furthermore, the entire complex was encased in a niched wall, reminiscent, once again, of the later Dynasty 3 Saqqara Pyramid wall.

The death of any Egyptian monarch was an important and historic occasion that took on even greater significance when it was coupled with the passing of one dynasty to the next. In the case of Khasekhemui (Fig. 10.8a), last king of Dynasty 2, his passage assumed special meaning. During his lifetime, Egypt retained much of its Predynastic flavour: crops were still grown much as they had been for a thousand years, writing was still in its infancy and architectural and artistic styles, although recognisably Egyptian, had yet to be codified or reach their final level of sophistication. Yet a generation after Khasekhemui was laid in his tomb, his successor, King Djoser, erected the Step Pyramid, the earliest known example of the now famous structure, inaugurating the glorious pyramid age. How such a transition could have occurred in about 20 years remains a mystery.

Like Menes's reign, Khasekhemui's occurs at a bridge or turning point for Egypt, and like Menes he is somewhat of a mystery to modern scholars. For example:

FIGURE 10.7 ◆ *The three-sided step* mastaba, *the architectural precursor to the first step pyramid at Saqqara.* Source: Courtesy of the Egypt Exploration Society

(a)

(b)

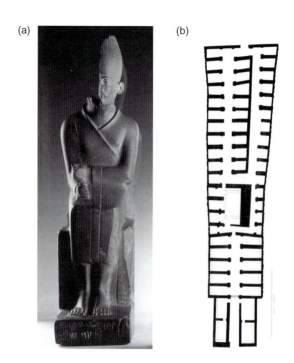

(c)

FIGURE 10.8 ◆ *Khasekhemui (a), tomb with its elongated form (b), multitude of storage chambers (c).*

(d)

FIGURE 10.8 ◆ (*continued*) *Khasekhemui's stone-lined burial chamber
(d) is quite different from all preceding* mastabas. *The massive mud-brick
wall that enclosed it mimics in size and structure the 'Fort of Khasekhemui'
at Hierakonpolis, depicted in Fig. 10.4. The* mastaba *and wall of Khasekhemui's
mortuary complex resemble in many ways the original plan for the Saqqara
complex of King Djoser.* Sources: (a) Scala/Art Resource, NY; (b) Brenda Coelho;
(c), (d) Courtesy of the Egypt Exploration Society

- Khasekhemui's official name was noted by both a traditional
  Horus name and the first use of the Seth name (because Seth
  represented Horus's nemesis, this is unusual);
- there is some question about whether the names Khasekhemui
  and Khasekhem represent one or two different kings;
- there is some implication that his reign was marked by civil war;
- he was buried at Abydos, but for some reason built a large
  mortuary temple at Hierakonpolis;
- he was the last king of his dynasty, yet his immediate successor
  may have been his son (which normally would have meant the
  continuation of his dynasty).

To trace his name, at the beginning of his reign the last king of the Second Dynasty adopted the Horus name Khasekhem, 'the power that appeared'. Later, however, he added the Seth-animal to the top of his *serekh*, and changed his name accordingly to the dual form Khasekhemui, 'the two powers have appeared'. Thus, current opinion holds that both names refer to the same king, rather than separate individuals – but why the need for a name change?

In the early part of his reign when his name appears as Khasekhem, he seems to have ruled only Upper Egypt – perhaps only the Hierakonpolis area. Indeed, his name is found but once outside this area. The Horus falcon usually found atop the king's *serekh* at this time wears only the white crown of Upper Egypt rather than the dual crown. Furthermore, stone vessels found at Hierakonpolis contain the ancient Egyptian word *bs* ('rebel') and accompanying remarks describe 'the year of fighting the northern enemy'. This evidence suggests that, when Khasekhem acceded to the throne, Egypt may have been divided by civil war and that his campaigns against the rebellious Delta resulted in a reunification of the country. To commemorate this achievement he may have changed his name to the dual form, Khasekhemui, to demonstrate he controlled both Upper and Lower Egypt; by placing Seth, a Delta symbol and mortal enemy of Horus, on his *serekh* he reinforced his claim as ruler of the entire Nile Valley, including the Delta.

At Abydos, Khasekhemui built an impressive mortuary complex that in design and symbolism is clearly a forerunner to the Step Pyramid at Saqqara. The *mastaba* and enclosure wall were a massive mud-brick structure that dominated the landscape (Fig. 10.8b). The burial chamber, for example, was lined with large blocks of dressed limestone (Fig. 10.8d), the first use of stone at such a large scale, and many buildings within the complex walls offer early examples of elements incorporated within the step pyramid complex. A second funerary enclosure constructed at Hierakonpolis was formerly thought to be a fort, but it remains a mystery. No one knows why it was built or what purpose it served (see Fig. 10.4a and b).

Textual evidence and archaeological evidence disagree on who succeeded Khasekhemui. The Abydos and Turin lists suggest there may have been a ruler between Khasekhemui and Netjerikhet, while archaeological evidence points to Netjerikhet as Khasekhemui's immediate successor: a sealing from Khasekhemui's tomb naming the mother of the king's

children, Nimaathap, lists Netjerikhet as one of her sons. Sealings of
Netjerikhet found in the tomb of Khasekhemui in turn suggest that
Netjerikhet oversaw the burial of his father, the preceding king, a role
usually reserved for the eldest son. Furthermore, ritual stone vessels recovered from both kings' tomb appear to be from the same manufacturer,
suggesting close proximity in time.

Netjerikhet is better known by his *nebty* name, Djoser, whose mortuary complex at Saqqara is the best-preserved early tomb complex and one
of the most impressive monuments in Egypt, representing a staggering
architectural achievement (Fig. 10.9). Within Djoser's 19-year reign, a
complex the size of a large contemporary town was created. Composed
of pavilions, terraces, ribbed and fluted columns, shrines, temples and
life-size statues, the Saqqara complex introduces for the first time many
funerary components that are expressed in later period tombs and temples. It should be noted, however, that the buildings and other structures
in the Step Pyramid complex, although beautiful and impressive, are not
a sudden and dramatic innovation. Rather, Djoser's complex is best
viewed as the culmination of a long tradition of funerary construction.

This magnificent feat was not, however, achieved without some hesit-
ancy: building plans were modified in mid-construction at least twice,
and it is clear that the capabilities of stone as a building medium were
not yet fully understood. Nevertheless, two distinguishing features of
the complex represent unique achievements in Egyptian architecture.
First, the monuments are built entirely of limestone, representing one of
the earliest examples of monumental stone architecture in the world.
Perhaps even more interesting, however, is that, although made entirely
of stone, the structure was built to look like perishable materials – mud
brick, reed bundles and palm logs – materials that were originally used
to build the earlier tombs. It almost seems as if the Egyptians were somewhat unsure of the properties of building in stone, so they mimicked
traditional building materials, knowing that they worked, and thereby
imparting some of that success into the new medium of stone – or they
made a conscious tribute to the past, but used stone, which they knew
would last longer. Regardless of the underlying reason, the stone blocks
used to construct the pyramid were made very small to mimic mud
bricks, and even the stone slabs forming the ceilings of passageways were
carved in imitation of rounded log beams like those that supported the

(a)

(b)

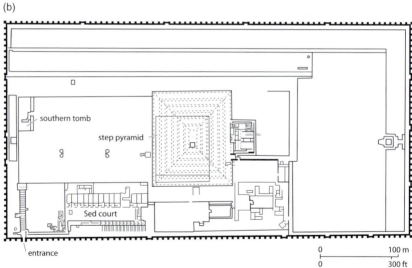

FIGURE 10.9 ◆ *King Djoser (a) and his Step Pyramid complex (b).*

Sources: (a) Jean Mazenod 'L'art de l'ancienne Egypte', Citadelles & Mazenod, Paris;
(b) After Brewer, Douglas J. and Teeter, Emily, *Egypt and the Egyptians*
(Cambridge University Press, 1999)

FIGURE 10.10 ◆ *The fluted columns at Saqqara are arguably among the most delicately crafted colonnades ever constructed in Egypt.*

Source: Photograph by D. J. Brewer

ceilings of earlier mud-brick tomb structures. These features are not replicated in the Fourth Dynasty when massive stone blocks were used in pyramid construction. A third interesting feature of the Saqqara complex is that many architectural elements, such as the jubilee court and the delicately fluted colonnade, appear here for the first and only time (Fig. 10.10).

Because it is so well preserved, the Saqqara complex provides information about the various components of the early royal mortuary complex, many aspects of which were retained in the next centuries. The focus of the complex is the pyramid tomb superstructure that rises in six steps to a height of 60 metres (197 ft) and is composed of 3,330,400 cubic metres of clay and stone (11,668,000 cubic ft). This superstructure was initially designed as a traditional flat *mastaba*, but for unknown reasons it was extended to the west and then converted from a flat *mastaba* to a stepped pyramid. It may be, as some have assumed, that its original design was always to be a pyramid but, in keeping with tradition, a *mastaba* was incorporated in the structure. Another possible motivation for using a pyramid shape is the fact that, situated within a large complex, the original *mastaba* could not be seen from afar. To make the intended political statement, it was raised to four and later to six steps or levels, thereby dominating the landscape.

But why build a pyramid? The best explanation probably lies in Egyptian ideology and religion. It was the king's wish that part of his soul (*akh*) ascend to the polar stars, which never set, and thus are eternal. Fifth Dynasty pyramid texts speak of the king ascending to the stars via a great staircase. The Step Pyramid, like so many other aspects of the mortuary cult, may symbolically have served as a staircase reaching to the heavens. On a more practical level, the desire to project royal power through a mortuary complex could only be met with an imposing structure that could be seen easily from a distance. The simplest large-scale structure to build, using available technology, was a pyramid.

Beyond the pyramid itself, the Saqqara complex comprises many other symbolic elements, each of which offers some insight into the Early Dynastic perceptions of the afterlife. Around the complex an enclosure wall was erected, decorated with recessed palace façade niching, identifying the royal nature of the site and emphasising it as the king's palace in the next world. The wall stood about 10.5 metres tall (34 ft) and enclosed 15 hectares (37 acres). The enclosure wall is decorated with 14 false gates, carved as if they were eternally open, perhaps emulating the walls of the ancient city of Memphis. A single functional door, 27 metres (88.6 ft) from the southeast corner and carved in the eternally open position, offers the only access into the complex (Fig. 10.11). Within the complex's walls were stations for performing the most important rituals of the king: a great court with a raised dais for receiving important visitors and tribute and a court for the *Sed* festival, which constituted a unique feature of the complex. The *Sed* festival was usually held every 30 years and represented the king's rejuvenation. The courtyard south of the Step Pyramid has two B-shaped platforms, which, as indicated by other representations of the *Sed* festival, were the turning marks for the king's ritual run. Further to the east stands the *Sed* court, lined on the east and west with three chapels emblematic of shrines of the north, the south and a combined form (Fig. 10.12). These buildings are reminders of what the now vanished Predynastic wood and mat shrines must have looked like. These ornate chapels are counterfeit – made only for the soul of the deceased king to enact the *Sed* ceremony. The doors, carved in an

FIGURE 10.11 ◆ *The single entrance to the Saqqara complex.*

Source: Photograph by D. J. Brewer

BOX 10.3 ◆ *Sed* festival

The *Sed* festival (also known as the 'jubilee') is known from the Early
Dynastic Period and was celebrated throughout Egyptian history. The
ritual was traditionally celebrated on the thirtieth anniversary of the
king's accession to the throne and thereafter at three-year intervals.
During the course of the festival, the king alternately donned the red
crown of Lower Egypt and the white crown of Upper Egypt and, grasp-
ing implements such as a slender vase, a carpenter's square and an
oar, ran a circuit between two B-shaped platforms. The king was then
symbolically enthroned. Because the central act of the ritual – running
the circuit – was physical, the *Sed* festival may be the vestige of a
Predynastic ceremony wherein the king proved his continued virility
and physical ability to rule. Although there is great emphasis upon the
celebration of the *Sed* in annals and autobiographies of courtiers who
served kings, little is known about the specific ceremonies.

FIGURE 10.12 ◆ *The* Sed *court bordered by three chapels, representing Upper Egypt, Lower Egypt and a combined form reflecting the unification of the two lands.* *Source*: Photograph by Patrick Richard Carstens

eternally open position, lead to blank walls – there is no interior space in any of the chapels.

The royal burial chamber was located 28 metres (91 ft) beneath the pyramid amid a warren of hallways and rooms, some of which are decorated with bright blue-green faïence tiles in imitation of woven reed mats (Plate 28). The burial chamber is lined with granite slabs quarried from Aswan, more than 950 km (590 miles) to the south. The king's body was carried into the subterranean passages through a descending entrance on the pyramid's north side. The burial chamber itself was entered through a hole in its ceiling that was later blocked with a massive granite plug. No body or coffin belonging to Djoser has ever been found and it is assumed that, like virtually all royal burials, the tomb was robbed in antiquity. Nevertheless, more than 40,000 stone vessels were discovered in the adjacent chambers of the substructure that once housed the burials of Djoser's family.

To the south of the pyramid was an elaborately decorated substructure, now referred to as the South Tomb (Fig. 10.13). The South Tomb's

FIGURE 10.13 ◆ *The mysterious Southern Tomb or Tomb of the Cobras at Saqqara.*
                                          Source: Photographs by D. J. Brewer

function is not known, but the energy expended upon its construction indicates that it was of great importance to the mortuary cult. Scholars have speculated that it contained the king's viscera or the king's placenta (saved from birth) or, more likely, was a repository for the king's *ka*.

The pyramid, its entrance, the offering chapel adjacent to the pyramid, the South Tomb and the enclosure wall were all standard features of later pyramid complexes. The *Sed* court, however, was never replicated in subsequent pyramid complexes.

Three other step pyramids, postdating Djoser's, are known to have been planned. The Sekhemkhet complex located southeast of Djoser's pyramid was originally envisaged as a seven-stepped pyramid, and its construction shows notable advances in stone architecture, most significantly the use of larger blocks that would have given the structure more strength and cohesion. Archaeological excavations at the site have been quite limited, but from the work that has been done it seems that the complex's subterranean foundation was completed, but that construction stopped in the early stages of work on the above-ground complex, probably because of the premature death of the king. At Zawiyet el-Aryan, about 7 km (4 miles) north of Saqqara, another pyramid had been planned, but even the substructure of this complex was left unfinished; however, it does appear that this was intended to be a five-stepped pyramid.

Mystery surrounds the builder and precise date of the last great step pyramid at Meidum (Fig. 10.14). Its initial phase of construction has been attributed to Huni, last king of the Third Dynasty, even though no contemporary inscriptions at the site bear his name. Like Sekhemkhet's unfinished pyramid at Saqqara, the Meidum Pyramid was originally planned as a seven-stepped tomb, but in a second phase of building it was enlarged to an eight-stepped pyramid. The more dramatic change converted it from a step pyramid to a true pyramid, and it is this innovation that links it with the Fourth Dynasty and the great pyramids of that period, the Dashur and Giza complexes. Like the later pyramid complexes, the Meidum complex included a small subsidiary pyramid to the south of the main pyramid (Fig. 10.15), a large rectangular enclosure wall surrounded the tomb and subsidiary structures, and a long causeway running from the pyramid to the valley served as an entrance to the complex. Unfortunately, the pyramid was doomed by faulty engineering:

FIGURE 10.14 ◆ *Although structurally flawed with the casing stones now lying around its base, the Meidum Pyramid still dominates the surrounding landscape.*

Source: Photograph by D. J. Brewer

FIGURE 10.15 ◆ *The small subsidiary pyramid of Meidum.*

Source: Photograph by D. J. Brewer

the facing was placed on loose rubble that filled the gaps between the steps, and in later years the foundation's unstable nature caused the casing to collapse. The rubble can still be seen today, fallen at the base of the pyramid. Nevertheless the Meidum Pyramid is an imposing structure, dwarfing earlier pyramids of the day.

Taken as a group, the step pyramids were not just tombs but were also deliberate propaganda statements. The pyramid's function was more than an elaborate resting place for Egypt's ruler; rather it was a means to memorialise the acts of the king as ideal expressions of national unity, prosperity and cultural achievement. They advertised and embodied the new state's objectives. They symbolised a break with the prehistoric past, yet also served to support the long-established reverence for the royal line of kings. The step pyramids, like later pyramids, represented a cross-section of Egyptian life. In a real sense, every factor of life intersected at the pyramids: labourers were needed to build the structures; farmers, fishermen and herders were needed to produce food; bakers and cooks prepared food for the workers; and tailors, tool makers, artists, scribes and virtually all other professions were called upon to complete these massive monuments in honour of the king.

Because a pyramid complex was essentially a political symbol, its location was important. The Saqqara Pyramid, located on a plateau at the apex of the Delta, across the river from Memphis, the new capital city, offered an excellent vantage point to relay its message of kingly power. The construction of the Saqqara Pyramid, like the later Giza pyramids, located 15 km to the north, involved *corvée* labour. Every Egyptian owed the state some form of tax, either as produce, product or labour. Naturally peasants could only offer their services, and many worked on state projects like pyramid construction. Thus when agriculture in the provinces was at a standstill because of the annual flood, each district supplied a quota of labour to the state for government-sponsored projects. Herodotus tells us that 100,000 men toiled on the Great Pyramid of Giza (although in reality the figure was probably more like 20,000). But even in Dynasty 3, building a step pyramid must have required thousands of workers. Workers had to be fed and clothed, so bakers and brewers were incorporated into the workforce, and fishermen, herders, farmers and craft specialists supplied tools and other staples to keep the workers healthy and productive. Grain collected through taxes was redistributed to brewers

BOX 10.4 ◆ Building a pyramid

How were pyramids built? Unlike the Dynasty 4 pyramids at Giza, Early Dynastic pyramids had stepped sides, thus their construction differed in a number of ways. Building any pyramid was in reality a huge landscaping project involving reconfiguring the land to accommodate the construction of many buildings, not just a pyramid, surrounded by a large wall.

The geometry of an Early Dynastic stepped pyramid is relatively simple: a square or rectangle placed one on top of another in a series of decreasing sizes. However, when building such a structure at a monumental scale, precision in placing the stones for each level was crucial. The question is: how was this level of precision met? How did the Egyptians control the rise and run of each of the steps on the Saqqara and later pyramids to ensure a stable structure? This was achieved by measuring the rise and run of each step and maintaining that distance throughout each level of the structure. Egyptian masons determined slope with a measurement called *seqed*, which was the amount (in cubits) of slope per cubit of rise. For example, if the rise (or pyramid step) was one cubit and the run was one cubit, the pyramid would have an angle of 45 degrees. By maintaining the same slope or *seqed*, the stability needed for massive architecture could be achieved.

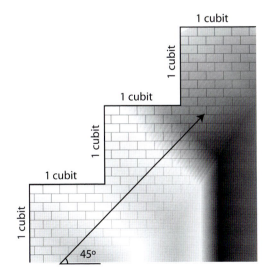

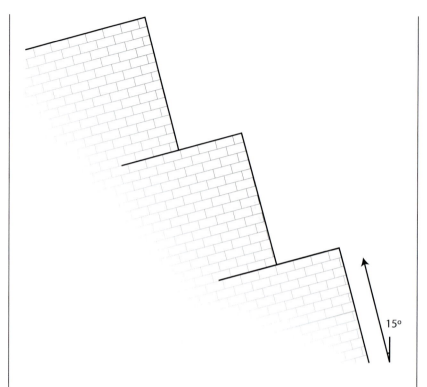

15°

Another feature of early pyramids was the method of building in accretions. When builders began Djoser's tomb they built a standard, albeit large, *mastaba*. When the transformation to a step pyramid began, they abandoned laying down horizontal beds of stone and began to build layers of brick that leaned inwards. That is, the sides of the Saqqara Pyramid, like other Dynasty 3 pyramids, were slanted slightly inwards (15°), which added stability to the structure. The stones used to build the Step Pyramid were made to imitate mud brick, so the hypothesised ramps used to build later pyramids had not yet come into play. Rather, the bricks, although heavy, could be managed by hand, without the use of complicated devices. The amount of time to build Djoser's Step Pyramid complex is debated, but it was certainly completed within the 19 years of his reign. Such an accomplishment would have required a large number of masons and labourers, the latter called to duty through the annual *corvée* system used throughout Egypt for community, national and other large-scale projects.

and bakers, warehouses of trade goods were tapped for elite offerings, and craft specialists – from stonemasons to potters to jewellers – were all employed to outfit the tomb.

Once completed, the public could bring offerings to the tomb in honour of the deceased king, thereby sustaining his soul; the public in turn believed that the deceased king would continue to bestow his favour upon them. In essence, the circle of life as it existed in the Nile Valley connected with the afterlife at the site of the mortuary complex. By sustaining the soul of the deceased king or a member of one's family, the living would be blessed by those in the hereafter, retaining the Egyptian balance between the two worlds.

As the Third Dynasty came to a close, Egypt was truly ready to evolve in all directions of society and government. The great pyramid age marks the most 'Egyptian' of Egyptian periods: the culture of the Old Kingdom is confident, secure and ingenious, art and architecture came of age, a cursive form of writing (Hieratic) was developed as a business script and the government established in the Early Dynastic Period became fully developed. All of what Egypt was to become – as well as its problems and eventual downfall – had its roots in the Predynastic and Early Dynastic Period, and from these Egyptian roots came the foundations for the later civilisations of antiquity.

BOX 10.5 ◆ Further reading

Hopefully this work has stimulated some interest in Egypt's formative period. For those readers who seek a more comprehensive and in-depth study of this period, I recommend the excellent work of Toby Wilkinson *Early Dynastic Egypt* and *The Prehistory of Egypt* by Béatrix Midant-Reynes.

Bibliography

Aldred, C. A. 1984. *Egypt to the End of the Old Kingdom*. London: Thames and Hudson.

Amelegos, G., D. van Gerven, D. Martin and R. Huss-Ashmore 1984. 'Effects of nutritional change on the skeletal biology of Northeast African (Sudanese and Nubian) populations'. In *From Hunters to Farmers* (ed. by J. Clark and S. Randt). Berkeley: University of California Press, pp. 132–146.

Baines, J. and J. Málek 1980. *Atlas of Ancient Egypt*. Oxford: Facts on File.

Brewer, D. J., D. Redford and S. Redford 1991. *Domesticated Plants and Animals: the Egyptian Origins*. Warminster: Aris and Phillips.

Brewer, D. J. and E. Teeter 1999. *Egypt and the Egyptians*. Cambridge: Cambridge University Press.

Brunton, G. 1928. *The Badarian Civilisation*. London: Quaritch.

Brunton, G. 1948. *Matmar*. London: Quaritch.

Butzer, K. 1976. *Early Hydraulic Civilizations in Egypt*. Chicago: University of Chicago Press.

de Cenival, J. L. 1981. *Un siècle de fouilles françaises en Egypte, 1880–1980*. Paris: IFAO/Musée du Louvre, p. 13 [no. 7 fragment bearing the name of King Aha-Menes].

Chmielewski, W. 1968. 'Early and Middle Paleolithic sites near Arkin, Sudan'. In *The Prehistory of Nubia* Vol. 1 (ed. by F. Wendorf). Dallas: SMU Press, pp. 110–191.

Debono, F. and B. Mortensen 1990. *El Omari: A Neolithic Settlement and Other Sites in the Vicinity of Wadi Hof Helwan*. Mainz am Rhein: von Zabern.

Diodorus Siculus 1989 (trans. by C. H. Oldfather). Cambridge: Loeb.

Dryer, G. 1992. 'Horus Krokodil, ein Gegenkönig der Dynastie 0'. In *The Followers of Horus, Studies in Honor of Michael Allen Hoffman* (ed. by R. Friedman and B. Adams). Oxford: Oxbow Press, pp. 259–263.

Dryer, G. 1992. 'Recent discoveries at Abydos Cemetery U'. In *The Nile Delta in Transition: 4th–3rd Millennium BC* (ed. by E. C. M. van den Brink). Tel Aviv: van den Brink, pp. 293–299.

Emery, W. B. 1949. *Great Tombs of the First Dynasty* Vol. 1. Cairo: Government Press.

Emery, W. B. 1954. *Great Tombs of the First Dynasty* Vol. 2. London: Egypt Exploration Society.

Emery, W. B. 1958. *Great Tombs of the First Dynasty* Vol. 3. London: Egypt Exploration Society.

Firth, C. M. 1927. *The Archaeological Survey of Nubia: Report for 1910–1911*. Cairo: Government Press.

Gammer Wallert, I. 1970. *Fische und Fischkulte im alten Ägypten*. Wiesbaden: Ägyptologische Abhandlungen 21.

Garstang, J. 1903. *Mahasna and Bêt Khallâf*. London: Egyptian Research Account.

Hassan, F. 1985. 'Radiocarbon chronology of Neolithic and Predynastic sites in Upper Egypt and the Delta'. *African Archaeological Review* 3: 95–116.

Hassan, F. 1988. 'Desertification and the beginning of Egyptian agriculture'. In *Akten des vierten internationalen Ägyptologen Kongresses, München 1985*, Band 2 (ed. by S. Schoske), pp. 325–331.

Herodotus 1990 (trans. by A. D. Godley). Cambridge: Loeb.

Hoffman, M. A. 1982. *The Predynastic of Hierakonpolis: An Interim Report*. Egyptian Studies Association 1.

Hoffman, M. A. 1984. *Egypt Before the Pharaohs*. London: Ark.

Hoffman, M. A., H. Hamroush and R. Allen 1986. 'A modal of urban development for the Hierakonpolis region from Predynastic through

Old Kingdom times'. *Journal American Research Center in Egypt* 23: 175–187.

Holmes, D. 1989. *The Predynastic Lithic Industries of Upper Egypt: A Comparative Study of the Lithic Traditions of Badari, Naqada and Hierakonpolis*. Oxford: British Archaeological Reviews 469.

Issawi, B. 1976. 'An introduction to the physiography of the Nile Valley'. In *Prehistory of the Nile Valley* (ed. by F. Wendorf and R. Schild). New York: Academic Press, pp. 3–22.

Kaczmarczyk, A. and R. M. E. Hedges 1983. *Ancient Egyptian Faience: An Analytical Survey of Egyptian Faience from Predynastic to Roman Times*. Warminster: Aris and Phillips.

Kaiser, W. 1964. 'Einige Bemerkungen zur ägyptischen Frühzeit III. Die Reicheinigung'. *Zeitschrift für ägyptische Sprache und Altertumskunde*, Berlin 91: 86–125.

Kaiser, W. and G. Dreyer 1982. 'Umm el Qaab: Nachuntersuchungen im frühzeitlichen Königsfriedhof'. *Mitteilungen des Deutschen Archäologische Instituts, Abteilung Kairo*, Wiesbaden 38: 211–269.

Lehner, M. 1997. *The Complete Pyramids*. London: Thames and Hudson.

Lee, R. 1968. 'What hunters do for a living, or how to make out on scarce resources'. In *Man the Hunter* (ed. by R. Lee and I. Devore). Chicago: Aldine, pp. 30–48.

Lovell, N. 1993. 'Anemia in the Nile and Indus Valleys: evidence and interpretations'. In *Comparative and Intersocietal Perspectives: the Indus Valley, Mesopotamia and Egypt* (ed. by R. Wright) (MS).

Manetho (trans. by W. G. Waddell). 1948. *Manetho*. Cambridge: Harvard University Press.

McHugh, W. P. 1974. 'Late Prehistoric cultural adaptation in Southwest Egypt and the problem of the Nilotic origins of Saharan cattle Pastoralism'. *Journal of the American Research Center in Egypt* XI: 2–29.

McHugh, W. P. 1975. 'Some archaeological results of the Bagnold-Mond expedition to the Gilf Kebir and Gebel Uweinat, Southern Libyan Desert'. *Journal of Near Eastern Studies* 34: 31–62.

Midant-Reynes, B. 2000. *The Prehistory of Egypt* (trans. by I. Shaw). Malden, MA: Blackwell.

Needler, W. 1984. *The Predynastic and Archaic Egypt in the Brooklyn Museum.* New York: Brooklyn Museum, Wilbour Monographs 9.

Oren, E. 1973. 'The overland route between Egypt and Canaan in the Early Bronze Age'. *Israel Exploration Journal* 23: 198–205.

Oren, E. 1987. 'The "Ways of Horus" in North Sinai'. In *Egypt, Israel, and Sinai: Archaeological and Historical Relationships in the Biblical Period* (ed. by A. E. Rainey). Tel Aviv: Tel Aviv University, pp. 69–120.

Parkinson, R. B. 1991. *Voices From Ancient Egypt.* London: British Museum Press.

Perrot, J. 1984. 'Structures d'habitat, mode de vie et environnement. Les villages des pasteurs de Beersheva, dans le Sud d' Israel, au IV millénaire avant l'ère chrétienne'. *Paléorient* 10: 75–96.

Petrie, W. F. 1901. *The Royal Tombs of the Earliest Dynasties* Part II. London: Egypt Exploration Fund.

Petrie, W. F. 1902. *Abydos* Part I. London: Egypt Exploration Society 22.

Petrie, W. F. and J. E. Quibell 1896. *Naqada and Ballas.* London: Quaritch.

Petrie, W. F., G. A. Wainwright and A. H. Gardiner 1913. *Tarkhan I and Memphis V.* London: Quaritch.

Quibell, J. E. and F. W. Green 1902. *Hierakonpolis II.* London: Quaritch.

Rice, M. 1990. *The Making of Egypt.* London: Routledge.

Rizkana, I. and J. Seeher 1987. *Maadi: The Pottery of the Predynastic Settlement.* Mainz am Rhein: von Zabern.

Roaf, M. 1990. *Cultural Atlas of Mesopotamia.* Oxford: Facts on File.

Saad, Z. 1947. 'The Royal Excavations at Saqqara and Helwan (1941–1945)'. In *Supplément aux Annales du Service des Antiquités de l'Egypte* Cahier 3. Cairo: IFAO.

Saad, Z. 1951. 'Royal Excavations at Helwan Cairo'. *Supplément aux Annales du Service des Antiquités de l'Egypte* Cahier 14. Cairo: IFAO.

Said, R. 1962. *The Geology of Egypt*. Amsterdam: Elsevier.

Seeher, J. 1990. 'Maadi eine prädynastische Kulturgruppe zwischen Oberägypten und Palästina'. *Prähistorische Zeitschrift* 65(2): 123–56.

Spencer, A. J. 1993. *Early Egypt*. London: British Museum.

Sponsel, L. 1989. 'Farming and foraging: a necessary complementarity in Amazonia', in *Farmers and Hunters: The Implication of Sedentism* (ed. by S. Kent). Cambridge: Cambridge University Press, pp. 37–45.

Testart, A. 1982. *Les chasseurs-cueilleurs ou l'origine des inégalités*. Paris: Société d'Ethnographie.

Vickers, W. T. 1989. 'Patterns of foraging and gardening in a semi-sedentary Amazonian community'. In *Farmers and Hunters: the Implication of Sedentism* (ed. by S. Kent). Cambridge: Cambridge University Press, pp. 46–59.

von der Way, T. 1986. 'Tel el Fara'in-Buto' 1. Bericht. *Mitteilungen des Deutschen Archäologische Instituts, Abteilung Kairo, Wiesbaden* 42: 191–212.

Wilkinson, T. A. 1993. 'The identification of Tomb B1 at Abydos: refuting the existence of a king Ro/*Iry-Hor'. *The Journal of Egyptian Archaeology* 79: 241–243.

Wilkinson, T. A. 1999. *Early Dynastic Egypt*. London: Routledge.

Wendorf, F. (ed.) 1968. *The Prehistory of Nubia*. Dallas: SMU.

Wendorf, F. and A. E. Marks 1975. *Problems in Prehistory: North Africa and the Levant*. Dallas: SMU.

Wendorf, F., R. Schild and A. E. Close (eds) 1980. *Loaves and Fishes: The Prehistory of Wadi Kubbaniya*. Dallas: SMU.

Winkler, H. 1938–39. *The Rock Drawings of Southern Egypt*. London: Egypt Exploration Society.

Index